Stay for Supper

Quadrille, Penguin Random House UK, One Embassy Gardens, 8 Viaduct Gardens, London SW11 7BW

Quadrille Publishing Limited is part of the Penguin Random House group of companies whose addresses can be found at global.penguinrandomhouse.com

Copyright © Xanthe Ross 2025
Photography © Ola O. Smit 2025

Published by Quadrille in 2025

www.penguin.co.uk

A CIP catalogue record for this book is available from the British Library

ISBN 978-178488-728-5
10 9 8 7 6 5 4 3 2 1

Publishing Director: Kajal Mistry
Commissioning Editor: Isabel Gonzalez-
    Prendergast
Copy Editor: Lucy Kingett
Designers: Hugo Ross & William Lyall
Photographer: Ola O. Smit
Props Stylist: Louie Waller
Food Stylist: Clare Cole
Food Stylist Assistants: Poppy Keywood
    & Martha Loving
Production Manager: Sabeena Atchia

Colour reproduction by p2d

Printed in China by C&C Offset Printing Co., Ltd.

The authorised representative in the EEA is Penguin Random House Ireland, Morrison Chambers, 32 Nassau Street, Dublin D02 YH68.

Penguin Random House is committed to a sustainable future for our business, our readers and our planet. This book is made from Forest Stewardship Council® certified paper.

Dedicated to Aphra, Cyra and Lyla

Stay for Supper

Xanthe Ross

Photography by Ola Smit

Quadrille

A BIT ABOUT ME

Food has always been a big part of my life. I was lucky enough that my mum made everything from scratch, from pies and puddings (desserts) to bread, so I never knew anything different. I grew up in a large household in rural Scotland – I'm one of six – so family meals were always very loud, busy and fun. I think my large appetite comes from meal after meal of striving to finish first so that I could make sure I got seconds before they went. Some of my strongest childhood memories are centred around the kitchen, with lengthy mealtimes waiting for everyone to finish, chaotic scenes and lots of cake baking, making a mess and licking of bowls. When I later moved to London, I wasn't excited about going to the pub with big groups of friends but was instead desperate to find something that made me feel passionate. I was drawn to food and started to make my way through books and documentaries about soil health, wheat, the global food system and chefs and food pioneers I admired such as Dan Barber, Michael Pollan and Nancy Silverton.

After reading so much about food and its impact on the world, I didn't fully understand if or how I could turn this growing passion into work, but I was willing to give it my best shot.

There were two pivotal moments for me. Firstly, I spent a few days in Cornwall with Dan Cox, an inspiring chef who had recently started his farm and was working towards opening a restaurant using the produce he grew. He was fermenting, making his own pottery, introducing heritage pig breeds and growing produce that worked with nature, not against it. I will never forget the feeling I felt on the train back to London after my trip, with a sack full of veg from the farm, muddy boots and a happy, smiling face. I was so inspired by Dan's work and how he was touching every aspect of the food he would go on to serve to his guests. I was also excited to return home to cook with produce that I had pulled from the ground myself.

The second influential event was taking part in a sourdough bakery class at E5 Bakehouse in East London, which triggered a still ongoing obsession with bread, flour and fermentation. I found just being in the bakery inspiring. E5's entire ethos is based on telling stories about well-sourced, local food through their baked products and the food they serve in their café. They mill their own flour from their farm in Suffolk, make their own jams and cordials, pay homage to other local farms' produce, waste as little as possible, bake everything from scratch – and do so with no unnecessary fuss or ceremony, simply just demonstrating how food can be showcased and celebrated. Again, my eyes were wide open after this experience, and I knew I had to be part of this world.

And so, my first attempt was to host a supper club. Supper clubs were then (in 2019) still quite a new concept in London, so I started out not really knowing what I was doing or what to expect from them. If you are new to them too, the concept is somewhere between a pop-up restaurant and a dinner party. Usually, supper clubs exist just for one night at a time, but sometimes hosts run them back to back as part of a series. They might have some form of theme to the night, or a kind of entertainment. My theme was, and still is, to showcase British produce and ingredients from suppliers I'd researched and whose stories I'd got to know. I hosted them at home, just for four to six friends, and asked them to contribute to the cost of ingredients while I cooked them a four-course meal. I began the supper clubs with very little cooking experience. I watched videos to learn techniques, read cookery books and tried new ways of doing things all the time. I was extremely dedicated to getting to know how to do everything I could. At the supper clubs, I acted as front and back of house, making and serving the food, and also as mixologist, making cocktails that mirrored the themes of the menu and serving wine to my guests. I laid the tables with linens and crockery I had begun to collect from antique markets around the UK and France and used flowers for the tables from local florists.

Around the time I was hosting my first supper clubs, I decided to quit my job in restaurant marketing in London. I knew there was something in the cooking and supper clubs that was worth pursuing. Before quitting, I booked to take part in a six week sustainable food course at Ballymaloe Cookery School in Ireland, somewhere I'd admired for a long time for its dedication to organic farming practices. Finding a course there that was so well fitted to everything that excited me about food felt almost too good to be true. The course not only consisted of classical cookery training but also time spent in the vegetable garden, milking cows, making cheese and attending lectures on food, farming and climate change. I thrived at Ballymaloe and was so grateful for the opportunity to live so close to nature, picking the vegetables for our dinner on the way home every night, being around like-minded people and swimming in the sea every morning at sunrise. My time there laid the foundations for not only the career that I wanted to pursue, but also the lifestyle that I wanted to live, too; being outside and being connected to the food I was eating.

The next obvious move was not to go back to London, but to move to Wales, where my family are from originally and my parents were living. My grandfather had left behind an incredible Victorian greenhouse that was overgrown and uncared for, so I spent weeks cleaning it out with the help of my dad and planting seeds for the season ahead. My knowledge was limited to what I'd learnt at Ballymaloe, but trial and error saw me through and I was captivated by the process of planting a seed and growing it into something I could eat. I bought laying hens, spent time learning to forage, made my own bread, signed up to an online pastry course and basically taught myself all that I could. I learnt so much during this time and look back so fondly on how this period established the way I see food, how I try to respect ingredients and how I cook. During this period, I was also using social media to tell my story, with a very small number of people following along. I talked them through my choice of seeds, mushrooms I'd found and cooked and how my hens were laying eggs in secret places around the garden. The audience grew slowly as I took them with me through adopting donkeys, cooking for my family and hosting supper clubs inside my greenhouse.

During this time, I did travel back to London about once a month as my boyfriend, Hugo (my now husband), was living there, as were many of my friends. Hosting supper clubs while I was there was a good enough reason to travel too, and I often brought produce that I'd grown in Wales to cook with. I hosted them in my parents' café in Notting Hill in the evening when it was shut, and then slowly went on to host them in venues around London. As my social media presence grew, so did a community who were interested in attending the supper clubs, and I was given the opportunity to host more. With the help of Hugo and my best friend, Jimmy, I naively dived headfirst into cooking for bigger groups, made a million mistakes along the way and fell in love with it. I found so much pleasure in witnessing the buzz of the room and the adrenaline rush that I got from hosting the events. I have always talked the guests through the menu at the beginning, even when it was just four of my friends attending, highlighting where I got the ingredients from and choosing particular kinds of menus according to what is in season.

While so much of what I learnt in Wales remains central to my work, after six years of living there I decided to move back to London so I could pursue the supper clubs full time. Living in London now, my message is just as important as it was when I started: to spotlight ingredients, suppliers and sustainable practices through delicious food served in a laid-back, fun and welcoming setting.

Since the early days, I have always found a thrill in the sense of community that my supper clubs create. I usually serve the food on long, communal tables so that groups are naturally intertwined. In a world where it is often challenging to find new and like-minded friends, this element of the supper clubs has become increasingly important to me. I actively encourage people to come alone and strive to create an environment where this is as normal as coming in a group. Meeting new people with a shared passion for food, and enjoying it in such a context, feels like the most natural way to socialise. Eating food together is a ritual that strengthens and upholds community in so many ways. Whether this is in a larger context, such as a supper club, or just at home with one or two others, food's ability to bring us together is something I try to never take for granted. It's a space for presence, conversation, or just silent reflection and enjoyment at the end of the day.

I want you to have fun cooking the recipes in this book, hosting and feeding yourself and those around you a full plate of nourishing, invigorating and, at its core, simple food.

HOW TO USE THIS BOOK

The recipes in this book are vegetarian, as are most of the dishes that I cook and serve at my supper clubs. I cook this way

because I want to demonstrate how inspiring vegetables can be when they are given the main stage, easily providing everything you need in terms of sustenance and satisfaction. Of course, we know the positive environmental impacts of eating less meat, too, so it feels important to be part of the movement to do so. Cooking and eating this way challenges me to come up with new ways to make vegetables interesting and it's so satisfying when I do. There are endless possibilities for demonstrating their variety and I hope you will see this too.

Stay for Supper is an accumulation of recipes I have cooked over the last few years that have changed and developed over time, as I have grown as a cook. I have served many of them at my supper clubs or for my family and friends. For every single one of my recipes, I lean on seasonal vegetables, crafted with simple techniques and add-ons that really elevate everyday dishes. Whenever I'm asked for advice about running supper clubs or hosting, my response is to lean on simplicity when you create the menu. I think the best cooking is that which gives ingredients the spotlight, through uncomplicated yet effective techniques.

I have always served food on big plates to be shared, whether I'm cooking at home or at my supper clubs. I've never worried too much about following a 'starter, main, pudding (dessert)' model. Instead, I serve the food as a consistent stream of dishes, usually accompanied by big bowls of bread to mop everything up, and always followed by pudding. I suggest following a similar style when you are serving many of the recipes in this book. Although the book is split into chapters, I hope that you will feel confident enough to weave the dishes together to create menus for yourself or for when you are hosting. Many of the condiments can be served on top of stews, the salads alongside the mains and the things on toast with a soup. I have provided suggestions alongside the recipes to help you pair them, but feel free to mix and match according to what you fancy. These simple moves fill my everyday eating with joy and satisfaction, and I hope they'll do the same for you.

PAIRING AND SCALING UP DISHES

I have given suggestions for pairing dishes together, both savoury and sweet, at the beginning of each recipe throughout this book. Of course, these are just suggestions to help you on your way, and these dishes lend themselves to being enjoyed independently as much as they do together, depending on the setting and quantity of people. My suggestions for pairings come from finding balance between flavours as well as which ingredients are in season at certain times of year and, according to that time of year, which kinds of dishes we might feel like eating together. I have given pudding suggestions in some places, too, in case you want to use the pairing suggestions to create an entire menu for your own dinner party or supper club.

The recipes can also be scaled up to cook for bigger groups. Simply multiply the quantities according to how many you are planning to feed – the recipes will all work being cooked this way. In terms of scaling down, the same rule can also apply, but if you are cooking for one, I would still consider cooking for two, or even four, to provide yourself with delicious leftovers the following day. While it's still worth taking time over a delicious recipe when cooking for one, you may as well use the opportunity to prepare another meal for yourself – two birds one stone!

For the cakes and meringue tower (page 166), instead of scaling up the ingredients, I'd recommend making two or three individual puddings as otherwise the cooking times can become a bit complicated.

If you're cooking for yourself, lean into how you're feeling on the day. It always changes and listening to yourself can be such a powerful tool. I encourage you to try to eat seasonally where possible, because produce not only tastes better when it's come from closer to home, but our bodies want and need different tastes and textures at different times of the year, to fuel us accordingly. A crunchy salad with an abundance of vegetables makes sense in the summer to cool us down, and a hearty, bean-based slow-cooked stew is the perfect partner on a freezing winter's day. My hope is that many of the recipes will be used to set you up with a refrigerator full of nourishing, exciting food for the week ahead or a weekend of hosting friends.

I hope that you will close *Stay for Supper* with the understanding of how much variety is possible within vegetarian cooking – and that you'll want to host more regularly.

TIPS FOR HOSTING

Presenting your food beautifully is of equal importance when cooking for yourself or hosting others. It truly elevates my enjoyment of eating when I've taken a couple of minutes to plate it nicely. So, my advice to you is this: just as you work on building layers of flavour into your food (more on this later), follow the same principle when it comes to plating, layer by layer. Of course, this doesn't refer to all the dishes, but it's beneficial to consider the structure of the final dish when plating anything. So, build strong foundations by cooking a delicious dish and after plating it, consider what might lift it up. For me, it's usually a fresh herb, either finely chopped or left as leaves, maybe yoghurt or crème fraîche, a drizzle of extra virgin olive oil, and always sea salt and a good grind of black pepper. Chives and parsley are my most-used herbs as a garnish, I always have a bunch of each in the refrigerator. Don't be afraid to play around to find your style. I will practise how I am going to plate a dish at least a couple of times before I serve it at a supper club so that on the night, with the added pressure, everything runs as seamlessly as possible.

I would also say that wherever you can, prepare elements of the dish, or the entire dish, in advance. Especially for the soups and stews chapter (page 48), as many of these dishes will actually benefit from being cooked the day before, allowing the flavours to develop further. This also means that if you are hosting, you'll have more time to focus on setting the table and being in a calm state of mind when your guests arrive. Preparing in advance even if you are just cooking for yourself or one other can make the process much easier.

SEASONAL STYLING IDEAS

Being a host is about so much more than just cooking. With a little bit of effort, you can create a really beautiful setting that doesn't have to cost a lot of money or take too much time. Once you have your core tableware, get confident with mixing and matching to create a beautiful tablescape. Once you start playing around, you'll find your own style. Don't feel that you need to buy new things each time you host. Explore charity shops and antique markets, invest is some good-quality cutlery and linens, do some research on local, sustainable florists (although dried flowers are a cheaper and more sustainable option, too) and the rest will follow. Don't be too precious about everything looking perfect and try to have some fun with it as the mood of the host definitely reflects the mood of the evening.

I love styling tables to reflect the menu and the time of year. In the spring I use bright table linens, lots of colourful

candlesticks and candle holders and specific flowers to reflect the feeling of new beginnings. I will use blossom, greenery and of course daffodils on the tables to reflect the feelings of hope spring always brings for the warmer, brighter months ahead.

In the summer I try to demonstrate the abundance of these months by using fresh produce to decorate the tables and a mixture of colourful flowers. Since local, sustainable ingredients are so important in my cooking I try to reflect these values when choosing the florals for my tables. The result is that the table reflects the season because I'm trying to use what is available to me relatively locally.

In the autumn (fall), a time that is still very abundant, I will move to more neutral tones that are reflected in nature at this time of year. I am a bit of a mushroom fanatic and so I try to get mushrooms, decoratively, on the table somehow and will go for cream or white candles and perhaps more of them, since the evenings will be darker.

In the winter, everything will be more pared back, with lots of candles and wintery smells. At my Christmas supper club in 2023, I had everyone stand up and do a giant cracker circle, pulling all at the same time. It was a fun way to get everyone together and cranked up the energy in the room for the rest of the evening.

Music is, of course, really important and again, with minimal effort can have maximum impact. A good speaker will go a long way, and a reliable playlist, too. In terms of lighting, I always dim the lights and lean on candles to do most of the work. Gentle lighting makes people feel confident and calm and harsh lighting can do the opposite. Even if you are only hosting a few people, I always think it's a really nice touch to write out a menu for your guests. This makes them feel more special in the same way that taking a bit of time over the table styling, the right lighting and a good playlist will. All these factors are of equal importance to the food you are serving when hosting or running a supper club.

Enjoyment is at the core of my belief when it comes to cooking and eating. I encourage you to give yourself the time and space to cook and to make a moment out of doing so. Treat yourself to beautiful produce once in a while, put music on, make a drink and don't rush the process. Being organised is essential to cooking and eating well, but a clean kitchen is good for the mind, too, so make sure you go into it tidily, and let the mess follow. I hope you enjoy these recipes as much as I have enjoyed creating them for you and I hope they inspire you to take time over making food for yourself and for those around you.

HOW TO COOK WELL

I have learnt, with practice, that cooking well can be really quite simple once you discover the right systems and structures to keep yourself on track. Understanding the importance of establishing these kitchen guidelines was essential to me being able to cook for large groups. I can now utilise the same set of tools to cook for myself and friends as I do for supper clubs. Being organised is key as it gives you time to optimise the flavour of each step of a recipe, resulting in a successful plate of food. My hope is that you will be able to use the tips I have outlined below as a checklist to create your own systems and structures to cook the best food you can and enjoy yourself while doing so.

TAKE YOUR TIME

Taking your time is a fundamental part of cooking well because flavours need a chance to properly develop. Onions that are cooked over a low heat for 10–15 minutes will start to sweeten and soften, but if you rush them, they'll be bitter and crunchy. What hope does your final dish have of succeeding if it begins like that? Reminding yourself that each step of the recipe is a building block to maximise the resulting flavour of the final dish will encourage you to take time over each part. Taking your time over cooking is also important from a ritualistic aspect, as it provides an opportunity to slow down during your lunch break, at the end of the day or on the weekend, focusing solely on the task at hand. This also helps you to see the process of putting together a dish as enjoyable in itself rather than just focusing on the final outcome. When hosting, the mistakes I make are always when I'm in a rush and haven't given myself the headspace to consider each part of what I'm cooking. If you are cooking for others, make sure you leave plenty of time to get everything done, and prepare what you can in advance. Good cooking is all about being well organised and giving yourself the time to complete each element of a recipe as though it were a dish in itself.

That being said, there are of course times when we need to quickly put together a meal. There are recipes in this book that satisfy those moments, such as Eggs and Soldiers with Asparagus (page 46), which I often have for supper or a Cheese Toastie with

Tomato Chutney (page 34), but I still value the opportunity to put everything else down and focus on putting a plate of food together for myself, even when the meal is very simple.

I suggest finding time every so often when you do have the energy to cook, such as quiet weekends or evenings, and scaling up your quantities to make dishes that can then last two or three days in the refrigerator. A little pot of Cannellini Bean and Parsley Dip (page 156) will be the perfect quick fix for days when you come in from work hangry and unable to wait until the main event. And a container of Crispy Breadcrumbs (page 155) will completely lift the simple tomato pasta you only had 10 minutes to put together. I cherish these quiet times, when I have no distractions and can just focus on the task at hand, and I hope you will give yourself that opportunity for pleasure too.

KEEP A TIDY KITCHEN

Before you start, make sure that you have clean surfaces, an empty dishwasher, nothing in the sink, washing up put away and nothing else blocking any of your kitchen space. It is true what they say: 'tidy kitchen, tidy mind'. Within reason, I would recommend washing up as you go to prevent feeling overwhelmed as you get to the end of your cooking. When I'm hosting, I will always try to do as much as possible before the guests arrive, as it makes the end of the night clean-down much more bearable. Enjoy the cleaning, too – it's can be really therapeutic to put on some loud music when everyone has left and dance around the kitchen finishing the dishes. My number one rule: never leave the washing up for the next morning! Going to bed with a completely clean kitchen will do wonders for your headspace the following day. In professional kitchens, the clean-down at the end of the shift is always taken very seriously and I try to emulate that in my own way, with washing up dried and put away, surfaces cleaned, floor swept and bins emptied. Trust me, it'll be worth it tomorrow.

WRITE PREP LISTS

I write many lists when I cook. They are very detailed, which means that ticking it all off as I go is satisfying. The lists start with everything I need to buy for the supper, followed by prep lists that include all the tasks I need to complete to put the meal together. For example, my list will be: buy lettuce, clean lettuce, make salad dressing, assemble salad. Often when hosting, your mind is working hard to remember everything you need to do, so preparing lists beforehand will mean you don't have to think too hard while you're cooking. I continue to write lists as I go through the afternoon and evening preparing everything, so that while my mind is ticking along trying to keep everything under control, I can rely on my piece of paper or my Notes app to do the remembering. Since I am now a practiced supper club host, it's become second nature for me to write these lists, regardless of whether I'm hosting a supper club or just cooking for friends at home. Be kind to your future self – no matter who you're cooking for. I love putting as much care into the meals I'm cooking for myself and friends as I would for my supper club guests; it's a small and rewarding kindness that makes everyday life substantially better, and it also sets up good habits for when you do host.

READ THE RECIPE

In one of her books, my friend Ella, founder of Deliciously Ella, says you should read a recipe through entirely before you begin cooking, and I think this is fantastic advice that I want to pass on to you. This really helps to properly understand how the dish is going to come together and each step's value in the final plate of food. You can then reread it as you go, but reading it through before helps you to engage with the whole process before you've even started. Throughout my journey, I have also learnt so many lessons by reading recipe methods and learning how different cooks do different things. So, even if you do not plan to cook a particular recipe, reading through it can provide new information that may help to guide you in your own cooking.

INVEST IN EQUIPMENT

Investing in a few good bits of kit in the kitchen is invaluable. Sharp knives will change your cooking and large chopping boards used with a damp cloth underneath to stop them sliding around while you chop will make the process more pleasurable, too.

I use a KitchenAid stand mixer for most puddings (desserts), pastries and anything that needs a good amount of mixing. I also use a Magimix food processor, which is a timeless piece of kit for anyone who likes to cook. I use a Dualit hand-held blender, which is especially good for blending soups, although there are many good brands of blender out there. A Microplane for grating or zesting, varied sizes of stainless-steel mixing bowls, a good peeler, a knife sharpener and a lemon squeezer are also things I reach for almost every time I cook. Second-hand platforms such as eBay are great for buying the more costly pieces of equipment, as many people sell tools for a fraction of the price with just very light wear.

I use 2 litre (2 quart) ice-cream tubs to store food that I've prepped ahead time, which can also act as storage containers for leftovers, and smaller round tubs for sauces and condiments. Always label your tubs to make everything is organised – masking tape and a Sharpie are my go-tos for labelling. Always put the date on the labels, too, so you can figure out when something needs to be eaten by. There are so many things we have to think about each day, so make one small thing easier for yourself to remember!

HAVE FRESH HERBS TO HAND

Leafy green herbs are perhaps my favourite ingredients for everyday cooking. They bring fresh, vibrant flavour to any dish you add them to, and when you're styling your food, a flash of green will almost always make a dish look more beautiful. A note, though: always mirror the flavours of the dish with the garnish. Herbs do add a strong flavour, so don't let their addition take away from the dish you've taken time to create just for the sake of making it look pretty. To keep herbs like parsley, mint, basil and coriander (cilantro) fresher for longer, take them out of the plastic (if they were bought like that) and store them in a small glass of water just as you would a bunch of flowers. I keep my bunches in the door of the refrigerator and every time I need them, I just pluck out a few stalks. You'll notice such a difference in how fresh they look and how long they keep by storing them like this.

Whether on a windowsill or in an outdoor space, it's also really easy to grow your own herbs. All you need is a small pot, and you can buy herb plants in any garden centre. Hardy herbs like rosemary, thyme and sage only need to be watered every couple of days, while basil, parsley and mint will probably need a drizzle most days. The only other thing you need to remember is to move the herbs into bigger pots as they start to grow bigger. Pick a couple that you use most frequently and start with those. Fresh mint tea made from mint you have grown is one of life's great pleasures.

BUY THE BEST OLIVE OIL YOU CAN

Good cooking starts with good-quality ingredients, and extra virgin olive oil is one of the most important, as it forms the base of so many dishes. Extra virgin is an unrefined, nutrient-dense olive oil that is not only better for you, but the flavour is so much deeper and stronger. Never be afraid to be generous with the amount of olive oil you use.

In a few of the recipes in this book, I call for rapeseed (canola) oil. I only use rapeseed oil when I'm cooking at a very high temperature because it has a higher smoking point than extra virgin olive oil, and so retains more of its nutrients when heated. It's also easy and less expensive to get high-quality, cold-pressed extra virgin rapeseed oil.

GO FOR ORGANIC EGGS AND DAIRY

Wherever possible, I will use organic and free-range eggs and dairy in my cooking. These are two industries in which animals are highly exploited and so where I can, I go for the best option to ensure I am supporting high animal welfare.

LEARN TO SEASON PROPERLY

Last but certainly not least, learning to season your food properly is undeniably the most important part of cooking. It's essential to add salt throughout the cooking process as well as right at the end when you're ready to serve. Salt affects the way that certain ingredients cook and deeply impacts the resulting flavour. Of course, you do not want to go completely overboard with the salt, so keep tasting as you go and add more salt if necessary, bit by bit. Constantly evaluating the flavours of the dish that you are putting together is a good habit to get into. I only use unrefined Maldon sea salt in my recipes. When it comes to pepper, I would suggest getting yourself a grinder and peppercorns so that you can grind it freshly onto your food. The flavour of the pepper is retained this way and carries itself more strongly through dishes.

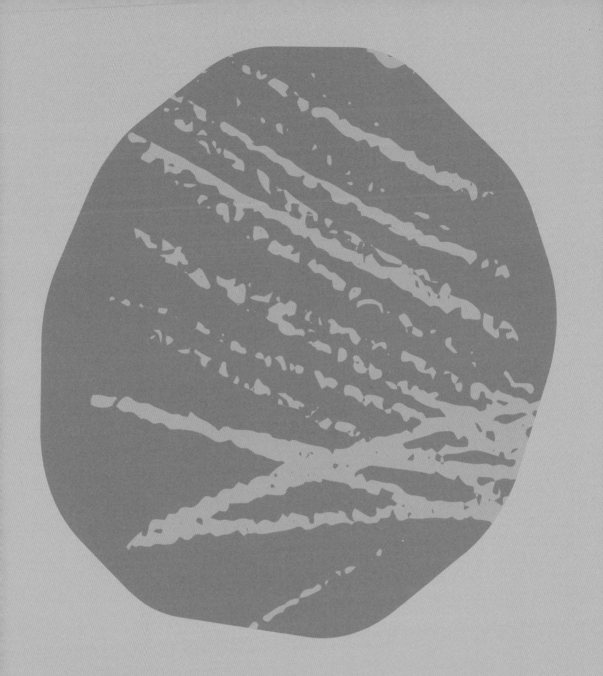

24–47

Things on Toast

My love of turning 'things on toast' into a meal came from learning to make bread in 2019. I took a course in London and brought my new knowledge home with me. I began to scratch the surface of an obsession with flour ratios, dough temperatures and shaping, and after that, bread became my main focus for a long time. I've read books, watched hundreds of videos and experimented with more loaves than you can imagine over the years. My fascination was timed perfectly, as my family swarmed home for lockdown in 2020, and there were suddenly many mouths to feed. The quantities of bread I was making meant that I had to dream up creative ways to use it, which resulted in regular 'things on toast' meals.

Baking instilled a new-found confidence in me when I started hosting supper clubs. From the beginning, I've served big bowls of bread throughout the meal, or started it with some form of 'things on toast'. From there, I began to experiment with new dishes and to host hundreds of people instead of the original four! Like most of the recipes in this book, I want to show you that this style of cooking lends itself to being pared down or elevated. Whipped Ricotta and Asparagus Bruschetta (page 37), for example, is the perfect solo weekday lunch, but make a few extra slices and present it slightly differently, and you have an ideal dinner party canapé. I believe that there is always an opportunity to satisfy yourself with a balanced plate of food when there's a loaf of bread around. I hope that you will use these recipes as inspiration to use toast as a canvas: sprinkle, lather, load and pile it high with whatever your heart desires.

Tomatoes on Toast

Tomatoes and toast are two of my favourite things in life, so when put together, they can't be beaten. I love this for lunch when I'm in a rush or even as a snack in the summer when I'm craving something fresh. I suggest making a big batch of the tomatoes and keeping it in the refrigerator for a day or so, as the tomatoes will break down and create delicious juices that'll keep adding flavour to this dish. I love to pile the tomatoes high on the toast, so I've been generous with the quantities in this recipe.

SERVES 4 PEOPLE

500g (1lb 2oz) ripe tomatoes, cut into eighths
½ bunch of fresh flat-leaf parsley, fine stalks and leaves chopped
juice of ½ lemon
1 tablespoon sherry vinegar
½ red chilli, deseeded and sliced
8 tablespoons extra virgin olive oil
4 slices of bread
1 garlic clove, cut in half
sea salt and freshly ground black pepper

GOES WITH
Warm Lentil Salad with Smoked Almonds and Feta (page 131), Confit Garlic (page 149), Courgette and Red Pepper Stew with Buffalo Mozzarella (page 71)

Put the tomatoes into a large bowl with the parsley, lemon juice, vinegar, chilli and 4 tablespoons of the olive oil. Season generously with salt and pepper and give it a good mix. Let the mixture sit for at least 10 minutes so that the tomatoes absorb all the flavour of the seasoning.

Toast the bread, then remove it from the toaster and rub each piece with the cut sides of the garlic and drizzle with olive oil.

Place on plates and top with the tomato mixture, spooning the juices over the tomatoes before enjoying straight away.

TIP: I always remove the calyx from the tomatoes when chopping them (the green part at the top that attaches the tomato to the plant) because getting it in a mouthful is never pleasant.

Baked Eggs

I used to make this all the time when I was living in Wales and didn't have much in the refrigerator. Having my own hens meant that I could rely on having fresh eggs pretty much whenever I wanted and could create a meal out of them with whatever I had in my pantry. Feel free to add spinach or any other leafy greens you have to the sauce at the end for some added nutrients.

SERVES 4 PEOPLE

2 tablespoons extra virgin
   olive oil
1 onion, thinly sliced
3 garlic cloves, very
   finely chopped
½ red chilli, sliced
½ teaspoon smoked
   paprika
200g (7oz) cherry
   tomatoes, halved
2 × 400g (14oz) tins of
   chopped tomatoes
2 tablespoons sherry vinegar
8 medium eggs
½ bunch of fresh flat-leaf
   parsley, leaves roughly
   chopped
sea salt and freshly ground
   black pepper
toasted bread, to serve

GOES WITH
Tomato Chutney (page 154),
Crispy Kale (page 144), Blood
Orange and Thyme Cake
(page 180)

Preheat the oven to 180°C (350°F).

Put the oil, onion and a pinch of salt into a large casserole dish (Dutch oven) and cook over a low heat for about 10 minutes until the onion is soft and translucent, stirring occasionally to ensure it doesn't catch.

Add the garlic, chilli and paprika and stir for a couple of minutes, then add the cherry tomatoes. Cook for a further 10 minutes, then add the chopped tomatoes, sherry vinegar and a generous pinch of salt and pepper. Increase the heat to medium and cook for a further 10 minutes.

Remove the pan from the heat and make eight indents in the sauce with the back of a spoon. Crack the eggs into the indents – don't worry if the indents aren't very deep and the eggs overflow a bit. Season the eggs with salt and pepper, then transfer to the oven and cook for 7–10 minutes, or until the eggs are cooked.

Remove from the oven and sprinkle over the chopped parsley, then serve immediately with the toast.

Wild Mushrooms, Butter Beans and Parsley Salsa on Toast

Mushrooms are arguably my favourite veggie ingredient because of the variety of ways in which they can be cooked. I think perhaps they are favoured by vegetarians because they can replace meat in a dish without having to rely on heavily processed fake meat substitutes. By nature, mushrooms have that meaty flavour and texture, especially when you start to explore wild ones, which are actually easy to find in most supermarkets these days. For this dish, I'd really recommend investing in a good mix of wild mushroom varieties, as they will elevate the dish to a new realm, I promise! However, it'll work with whatever mushrooms you have access to.

SERVES 4 PEOPLE

2 tablespoons extra virgin olive oil
4 garlic cloves, roughly chopped
400g (14oz) mixed wild mushrooms, cleaned and chopped into similar sizes (as big as the smallest mushroom)
2 × 400g (14oz) tins of butter (lima) beans, drained and rinsed
70ml (2½fl oz/5 tablespoons) white wine
100ml (3½fl oz/scant ½ cup) vegetable stock
sea salt and freshly ground black pepper
4 slices of bread, toasted or grilled

FOR THE PARSLEY SALSA
bunch of fresh flat-leaf parsley, leaves picked
3 tablespoons capers
zest of 1 lemon, plus juice of ½
½ teaspoon Dijon mustard
6 tablespoons extra virgin olive oil

Put the oil, garlic and mushrooms into a saucepan over a low heat and season with salt and pepper. Cook for about 5 minutes, then add the butter beans along with the white wine and stock. Season again, then increase the heat to medium. Simmer for about 10 minutes, stirring occasionally, until the beans have softened and the sauce has reduced slightly.

Meanwhile, make the parsley salsa. Bunch the parsley leaves together under one hand, then shred them finely with a sharp knife using swift individual motions. Cutting the parsley delicately preserves its flavour (this is the same for basil and other soft herbs). Roughly chop the capers so that they are about the same size as the parsley leaves, then combine them both in a bowl with the remaining ingredients. Mix everything together and taste it to check the seasoning, adding more salt and pepper if you think it needs it. Alternatively, combine everything in a food processor and pulse until it has reached your desired consistency.

Once everything is ready, pile the beans and mushrooms on top of the toast or grilled bread, then drizzle over a spoonful of parsley salsa and enjoy immediately.

GOES WITH
Leeks with Roasted Garlic and Walnut Sauce (page 140), Labneh with Roasted Tomatoes (page 139)

Cheese Toastie with Tomato Chutney

While most of my recipes are very vegetable heavy and quite fresh, I had to include a recipe for a cheese toastie because I think there is little on this planet that is more comforting. On its own, sometimes it's all I need, but it is also perfect paired with fresh tomato chutney and a green salad, or served on the side of a bowl of freshly made soup. This cheese toastie has lifted me out of a funk on many occasions and I hope it will do the same for you.

SERVES 4 PEOPLE

8 thin slices of bread
20g (¾oz) unsalted butter
280g (10oz) mature Cheddar,
  thinly sliced
2 tablespoons Tomato
  Chutney (page 154)

GOES WITH
*Roasted Tomato, Thyme
and Butter Bean Soup (page
62), Hugo's Gem Lettuce
Caesar Salad (page 126),
No-churn Raspberry Ice
Cream (page 162)*

Preheat the oven to 180°C (350°F).

Toast the slices of bread, then butter them on one side. Lay the slices butter-side down on a board and cover the unbuttered sides with the cheese.

Transfer the slices to a baking tray (pan) lined with baking parchment, then cook in the oven for 5 minutes. Once the cheese has melted, remove the cheese on toast from the oven and spread a teaspoon of tomato chutney on four of the slices. Then, sandwich the slices together so that each sandwich uses one slice spread with chutney, using the cheese on each slice as glue to stick the slices together. Return the sandwiches to the oven for a further 3–5 minutes until oozing and golden, then remove from the oven and allow to rest for a minute before slicing in half and serving.

Whipped Ricotta and Asparagus Bruschetta

I was inspired to cook asparagus this way after trying a dish at the very beautiful Atelier September in Copenhagen. They served the asparagus cut into rounds like this and I've done it a lot since. The British asparagus season is so short that I try to cook with them every day when they're around. This means that later in the season, I may be searching for ways to cook them that keep me inspired. Something simple like cutting them differently satisfies that for me, and I love the delicacy it gives to the asparagus. Asparagus always matches beautifully with dairy because of its freshness.

SERVES 4 PEOPLE

200g (7oz) ricotta
zest and juice of ½ lemon
2 tablespoons extra virgin
olive oil
2 × 250g (9oz) bunches of
asparagus
4 slices of bread, toasted
sea salt and freshly ground
black pepper

GOES WITH
*Lentil and Mushroom
Bolognese (page 82), Squash,
Tahini, Crispy Sage and
Hazelnuts (page 118), Leeks
with Roasted Garlic and
Walnut Sauce (page 140)*

Put the ricotta, lemon zest and juice, 1 tablespoon of the olive oil, a sprinkle of salt and a generous grind of pepper into a bowl. Whisk until smooth and light.

Snap the woody ends off the asparagus, then cut them into 1cm (½ inch) rounds. Fill a bowl with cold water and ice and set it to one side.

Bring a large saucepan of generously salted water to the boil, then drop in the asparagus pieces and cook for about 1 minute. You want the asparagus pieces to remain crunchy, so be careful not to overcook them. Drain and transfer straight to the ice bath. This will stop the cooking and also help the asparagus keep their fresh green colour.

Cut the slices of toast in half and lay them on a plate. Spoon some of the ricotta onto each piece, then use the back of your spoon to spread it across the toast.

Drain the asparagus and pat them gently dry with a dish towel. Put them into a bowl, drizzle with the remaining olive oil and season with salt and pepper. Mix gently, then top the whipped ricotta with a generous spoonful of the dressed asparagus. Season again if you like, then serve immediately.

Broad Beans and Peas on Toast

If you're looking to put together a very quick lunch that's also full of nutrients and delicious, this is the one for you. I love the freshness of the peas and beans with the summer herbs, but you could make it at any time of year, given that frozen vegetables are always available.

SERVES 4 PEOPLE

200g (7oz) frozen broad
(fava) beans
200g (7oz) frozen peas
juice of 1½ lemons, plus
zest of 1
4 tablespoons extra virgin
olive oil
½ bunch of fresh mint,
leaves picked
½ bunch of fresh basil,
leaves picked
1 heaped tablespoon
cream cheese
1 tablespoon cold water
4 slices of bread, toasted
sea salt and freshly ground
black pepper

GOES WITH
*Crunchy Bean and Summer
Veg Salad (page 123), Pickled
Summer Veg (page 146)*

Bring two saucepans of generously salted water to the boil and cook the broad beans for 4 minutes and the peas for 2 minutes, then drain them both and refresh under cold water to stop the cooking process.

Put the beans and peas into a food processor along with the lemon juice, oil, mint, basil, cream cheese and cold water. Season well with salt and about ten grinds of pepper, then pulse until the mixture is a chunky, nicely textured consistency.

Top the toast with the pea and bean mixture, an extra pinch of sea salt and pepper and the lemon zest, then serve.

Baked Beans on Toast

This is one of the first recipes I ever wrote. It's become a staple with my family when we are together, and they all now cook it when they're with their own families at home too. The beans keep well for a couple of days, so this is a perfect dish to make to make for workday lunches. For me, it provides just the right level of satisfaction: full but not lethargic. For added oomph and satisfaction, you could top the beans with a fried egg, a good grating of Parmesan or a vegetarian alternative.

SERVES 4 PEOPLE

2 tablespoons extra virgin
  olive oil
1 onion, roughly chopped
3 garlic cloves, very finely
  chopped
1 tablespoon tomato
  purée (paste)
3 × 400g (14oz) tins of
  cannellini beans
2 × 400g (14oz) tins of
  chopped tomatoes
1 tablespoon balsamic
  vinegar
2 tablespoons red
  wine vinegar
1 tablespoon dark soy sauce
1 teaspoon clear honey
4 slices of bread, toasted
handful of grated Parmesan
  or Cheddar cheese,
  to serve
sea salt and freshly ground
  black pepper

GOES WITH
*Caramelised Leeks, Toasted
Walnuts and Fried Eggs
on Toast (page 42), Crispy
Kale (page 144), Apple and
Blackberry Pie (page 169)*

Put the oil, onion and a pinch of salt into a saucepan large enough to hold all the ingredients. Cook over a low heat for about 10 minutes until the onion is soft and sweet, stirring occasionally to ensure it doesn't catch. Add the garlic and cook for a further 5 minutes or so until it's translucent.

Add the tomato purée and mix everything together, then add the remaining ingredients, increase the heat to medium and season with salt and pepper. Give it a good stir, then leave to cook for about 20 minutes until the sauce has reduced and thickened. Taste the beans to check you are happy with the seasoning, then remove from the heat.

Pile a generous spoonful onto each slice of toast and serve topped with grated Parmesan or Cheddar cheese.

Caramelised Leeks, Toasted Walnuts and Fried Eggs on Toast

This recipe is a prime example of how exciting simple food can be, and how you can mix up the ingredients that you probably already have at home to create something fresh that will keep weekday meals interesting. A chef I once worked with introduced me to caramelised leeks on toast, and I'm endlessly grateful to him for that. The leeks are also delicious with burrata, so if you wanted to turn this into a starter when hosting, you could replace the eggs with burrata.

SERVES 4 PEOPLE

25g (1oz) unsalted butter, plus extra for spreading and 10g (½oz) for frying (optional)
5 tablespoons extra virgin olive oil
6 leeks, trimmed and sliced into 2cm (¾ inch) rounds
2 tablespoons crème fraîche
60g (2oz) walnut halves
4 medium eggs
4 slices of bread, toasted (rye works nicely)
sea salt and freshly ground black pepper

GOES WITH
*Confit Garlic (page 149),
Poached Pears with Cream
(page 174)*

Heat the butter and 4 tablespoons of the oil in a heavy-based frying pan over a low heat, then add the leeks and a generous pinch of salt. To properly caramelise the leeks, you need to cook them slowly over a low-medium heat for about 40 minutes. Stir them occasionally so that they don't catch, and make sure they're spread relatively evenly across the bottom of the pan. If the leeks start to colour too much, add a splash of water and turn down the heat. Once the leeks are cooked, stir through the crème fraîche, and remove the pan from the heat.

Meanwhile, preheat the oven to 180°C (350°F).

Put the walnuts onto a baking tray (pan) and toast them in the oven for about 5 minutes until they are slightly golden, but keep a close eye on them. Remove them from the oven and allow to cool, then chop them into small pieces. You want them to almost crumble over the leeks at the end.

Once the leeks and walnuts are ready, it's time to fry the eggs. The key to good fried eggs is a nice hot pan. This will mean that the whites fully cook and you won't be left with that gloop that sometimes remains on top. Of course, you should be careful not to get the pan too hot or the eggs will burn. Place a frying pan over a high heat and allow it to heat up for about 2 minutes. Hold your hand 10–15cm (4–6 inches) above the centre of the pan (being careful not to touch it) and if you can feel the heat, it's hot enough to cook the eggs. Drizzle the remaining tablespoon of olive oil (or unsalted butter if you prefer) into the pan and crack the eggs in one by one. Season with salt and pepper and cook until the whites are set.

Butter the toast and spread with a generous helping of the leeks. Sprinkle with the chopped walnuts, then top each piece of loaded toast with an egg and season with more salt and pepper.

Roasted Aubergine, Tahini Sauce and Cucumber Salsa on Toast

This recipe is a good example of something that makes a simple, quick lunch but also an exciting starter or snack when you're hosting. Cut up the toast into small bite-sized pieces to make a canapé-style starter or make all the elements, keep them in containers and have them for lunch throughout the week. The tahini sauce goes with so many different things. I make it all the time and drizzle it on just about anything, so don't be afraid to take it to other places.

SERVES 4 PEOPLE

3 aubergines (eggplants)
extra virgin olive oil, for
    drizzling
sea salt and freshly ground
    black pepper
4 slices of bread, toasted
1 red chilli, finely sliced

FOR THE CUCUMBER SALSA
1 cucumber, peeled and
    diced into 1cm (½ inch)
    cubes
juice of 1 lemon
2 tablespoons extra virgin
    olive oil
generous handful of mint
    leaves, thinly sliced, plus
    extra to serve

FOR THE TAHINI SAUCE
2 tablespoons tahini
2–3 tablespoons cold water
¼ teaspoon clear honey
juice of ½ lemon

GOES WITH
*White Miso Butter Beans
(page 65), Cold Noodle
Salad with Tahini and Miso
Dressing (page 92), No-churn
Raspberry Ice Cream (page
162)*

Preheat the oven to 210°C (410°F). Cut the tops off the aubergines, then cut them in half lengthways and slice the flesh horizontally at 1cm (½ inch) intervals, being careful not to slice through the skin. Drizzle a couple of tablespoons of olive oil over the top and season with salt and pepper. Place the aubergines flesh side up on a baking tray (pan) and roast in the oven for about 45 minutes, or until they are very soft.

While the aubergines cook, you can prepare everything else. I'd suggest making the cucumber salsa first because it will develop more flavour as it sits in its juices. Put the cucumber into a bowl along with the lemon juice, olive oil, mint leaves and some salt and pepper. Mix everything together, then set aside.

To make the tahini sauce, spoon the tahini into a bowl and add the water. Whisk with a fork until you have a smooth paste, adding more water if you'd like your sauce to be thinner. Add the honey and lemon juice, then season everything with salt and pepper. Whisk to combine, then taste to check you're happy with the seasoning.

Once the aubergines are very soft, take them out and let them cool down a bit. Once they're cool enough to handle, scoop out the flesh into a bowl. Spread a spoonful of the tahini sauce on the slices of toast, followed by a spoonful of the aubergine, then top with the cucumber salsa. Finish with a few fresh mint leaves, sliced chilli and enjoy.

Eggs and Soldiers with Asparagus

Eggs and soldiers is my comfort meal – it would be my last meal on Earth. I don't think it should be limited to just breakfast because it's the perfect supper when you don't have the energy or time to cook something more complex. Nothing used to satisfy me more than picking up eggs from my hens, making a loaf of sourdough from scratch and buying a packet of butter that was made from the milk of the cows that I could see from my house. It's the epitome of local eating and it makes my heart full to have sourced all my food from within walking distance.

This is, of course, the simplest of recipes, but I do think there are a couple of knacks to making the perfect eggs and soldiers, which I explain below. When the British asparagus season comes, speedily as it does, I could not think of a better way to eat asparagus other than dipped into eggs. As ever, the higher the quality of the ingredients, the better it's going to turn out.

SERVES 4 PEOPLE

8 medium eggs (the fresher
   the better)
250g (9oz) asparagus
4 slices of your favourite
   bread
20g (¾oz) unsalted butter,
   plus extra for spreading
sea salt and freshly ground
   black pepper

GOES WITH
*Roasted Tomato, Thyme and
Butter Bean Soup (page 62),
Chocolate Chip and Almond
Butter Cookies (page 165)*

If you keep your eggs in the refrigerator, take them out to come to room temperature a few hours before you want to make this dish. If the eggs are too cold when they touch the boiling water, they'll crack immediately.

Snap the woody ends off the asparagus and add them to the water. Cook the asparagus for 2–3 minutes. While the asparagus is cooking, put the bread into the toaster.

Once the asparagus is cooked, drain and put it into a bowl with the butter and a good pinch of salt. Mix gently, so the butter melts and covers the asparagus.

Bring a saucepan of salted water to the boil, then reduce the heat to a simmer and carefully add the eggs using a ladle or a big spoon. If you drop the eggs in with your fingers, you risk them falling to the bottom and cracking. Cook for 5½ minutes (set a timer!), then place into your egg cups.

Butter the toast, then cut it into 1cm (½ inch) soldiers and season with salt and pepper. Put the eggs into egg cups, take off the tops with a knife and season with salt and pepper. Divide the soldiers and the buttery asparagus between the plates, add the eggs in their egg cups, and dip to your heart's content!

48–77

Soups and Stews

Most of the soups and stews in this chapter are on regular rotation in my kitchen throughout the year. I love that by taking my time, I can build so much flavour into them. Good soups and stews usually start with a base of onions and/or garlic, then maybe celery, carrots and fresh herbs. Then you build on that foundation with other vegetables, beans, more herbs, stock, acidity and plenty of seasoning. When all these layers are focused on individually and are properly considered, you know you'll be left with a delicious dish.

Soups and stews are great when you need to multitask, as you can get on with something else while the pot slowly bubbles away on a low heat. The following recipes are perfectly suited to stocking up your refrigerator with filling and nutrient-dense meals for the week, but they also work brilliantly as dishes for a sprawling lunch at the weekend if you're hosting. When I cook lunch for friends, I often serve stews alongside salads, dips and bread, so it really feels like a generous spread. Small additions like pesto on top can really elevate an understated dish. When it comes to serving, I recommend some fresh herbs on top, or a dollop of yoghurt and a drizzle of extra virgin olive oil also goes a long way.

Squash, Carrot and Miso Soup

I started making this soup at university to serve to friends on cold winter evenings and it has stuck with me ever since. I love the addition of miso, which adds umami flavour to the natural sweetness of squash and carrots. This is a lovely, hearty soup that is actually very simple to put together. I like to serve this soup quite thick, but if you'd prefer it thinner, then please feel free to add a little more vegetable stock.

SERVES 4 PEOPLE

1 butternut squash, peeled, deseeded and chopped into 2cm (¾ inch) pieces
4 carrots, peeled and chopped into 2cm (¾ inch) pieces
extra virgin olive oil, for cooking
1 onion, diced
1 thumb-sized piece of fresh ginger root, peeled and roughly chopped
4 garlic cloves, roughly chopped
½ red chilli, thinly sliced (optional)
400ml (14 fl oz/generous 1½ cups) coconut milk
400ml (14 fl oz/generous 1½ cups) vegetable stock (or more, depending on the consistency you like)
2 tablespoons white miso paste
1 tablespoons rice vinegar
sea salt and freshly ground black pepper
coconut yoghurt, to serve
coriander (cilantro) leaves, to serve (optional)

GOES WITH
Crispy Kale (page 144), Herb Butter (page 147), Poached Pears with Cream (page 174)

Preheat the oven to 220°C (425°F).

Put the squash and carrots into a roasting tin, drizzle with olive oil and season with salt and pepper. Roast in the oven for about 30 minutes, or until soft.

Put the onion into a large heavy-based saucepan along with a couple of tablespoons of olive oil and a pinch of salt. Cook over a low heat for 10–15 minutes until the onions are soft, stirring occasionally to prevent them catching. Add the ginger, garlic and chilli, if using, and cook for another couple of minutes until the garlic is translucent.

Add the coconut milk and increase the heat to bring it to a simmer. Once the squash and carrots are soft, scrape them into the pan, then add the vegetable stock. Check the seasoning, adding more salt and pepper if needed, then let everything simmer for a few minutes to allow the flavours combine.

Remove the pan from the heat and let the soup cool slightly, then add the miso paste and vinegar and stir them into the soup (if you add the miso paste while the soup is too hot, you may damage some of the good bacteria in the miso that is healthy for your gut).

Use a hand-held blender to purée the soup, then serve it with a dollop of coconut yoghurt and some coriander leaves, if using.

Burnt Courgette, Basil and Cannellini Bean Stew

This recipe is so simple but effective. It's the type of cooking that doesn't need many ingredients, instead letting the ones you do use shine. I first made this for my family in France in the summer, with courgettes (zucchini) and basil straight from the garden, and I've made it so many times since. When we are on holiday, we eat feasting-style most nights, with lots of different dishes making up the meal, and everyone contributing their own bit of the supper. This was the result of one of those nights. Usually there will be some kind of protein cooked on the fire for those who want it, then lots of delicious vegetarian dishes making up the rest of the meal.

SERVES 4 PEOPLE

6 courgettes (zucchini), quartered lengthways, then chopped into 2cm (¾ inch) pieces
3 tablespoons extra virgin olive oil, plus extra for drizzling
8 garlic cloves, thinly sliced
3 × 400g (14oz) tins of cannellini beans
600ml (21 fl oz/generous 2 cups) vegetable stock
30g (1oz) fresh basil leaves, shredded
juice of 1 lemon
¼ bunch of fresh flat-leaf parsley, leaves roughly chopped
sea salt and freshly ground black pepper

GOES WITH
Crispy Breadcrumbs (page 155), Tomatoes on Toast (page 28), Peach, Hazelnut and Basil Galette (page 183)

Add the courgettes to a saucepan with the extra virgin olive oil over a medium heat for about 15 minutes, or until charred. Once charred, add the garlic and a generous pinch of salt and continue to cook for a further 10–15 minutes until the courgettes are very soft and have started to caramelise. Season generously with salt. If they start to burn, add a splash of water and reduce the heat slightly before increasing it again.

Once the courgettes are ready, drain and rinse the beans and add them to the pan along with the vegetable stock. Stir gently and reduce the heat. Season again, then let everything cook for about 20 minutes, until some of the liquid has evaporated and the stew has a slightly creamy consistency.

Remove the stew from the heat and add the basil and lemon juice, stirring to combine. Finish with a drizzle of olive oil and the chopped parsley to serve.

Coconut and Mushroom Broth with Soba Noodles

This broth is ideal for the colder months as it is warming and satisfying. I've gone with carrots and broccoli, but you could use any vegetables you have. I try to always have a green vegetable here and broccoli works well, but I've also tried cavolo nero (lacinato kale), asparagus and green beans before, so use whatever takes your fancy. In whichever form, this is made on repeat in my house when I am in need of something soothing and easy.

SERVES 4 PEOPLE

1 tablespoon sesame oil

1 thumb-sized piece of fresh ginger root, peeled and grated

2 garlic cloves, very finely chopped

2 spring onions (scallions), thinly sliced, plus extra to serve

800ml (27 fl oz/3⅓ cups) coconut milk

500ml (17 fl oz/generous 2 cups) vegetable stock

330g (11½oz) soba noodles

4 medium eggs

2 tablespoons miso paste dissolved in 50ml (1¾ fl oz/3½ tablespoons) water

200g (7oz) chestnut (cremini) mushrooms, sliced

2 carrots, peeled and sliced into 5cm (2 inch) rounds

1 broccoli, chopped into small florets

TO SERVE (OPTIONAL)
sesame seeds
¼ bunch of fresh coriander (cilantro), leaves picked

Put the sesame oil, ginger, garlic and spring onions into a saucepan and cook over a low heat for a few minutes, stirring constantly, then add the coconut milk and stock. Increase the heat to medium and let the broth simmer for 15–20 minutes until aromatic.

Meanwhile, bring a large saucepan of salted water to the boil and cook the noodles according to the packet instructions. Drain the noodles and refresh under cold water, then set aside.

Bring another saucepan of salted water to the boil and carefully add the eggs using a ladle or a spoon. Boil the eggs gently for 6 minutes, then remove them and run them under cold water. When they are cool enough to handle, peel them and set aside.

Once the broth has been simmering for long enough, remove it from the heat. Stir the miso and water mixture into the broth, then add the mushrooms, carrots and broccoli. Cover the pan and let it sit for a few minutes. The heat of the broth will cook the vegetables while keeping them crunchy and not killing the beneficial bacteria in the miso.

Divide the noodles between the bowls and ladle over the broth and vegetables. Halve the eggs and add two halves to each bowl, then sprinkle with sesame seeds, spring onions and a few coriander leaves.

GOES WITH
Roasted Aubergine, Tahini Sauce and Cucumber Salsa on Toast (page 45), Chocolate Chip and Almond Butter Cookies (page 165)

Smoked Tofu in Tomato and Olive Sauce

This dish is the perfect lunch for a weekday when you don't have much time or many ingredients in the kitchen. Smoked tofu is really worth getting your hands on if you can (I love the Tofoo one), as it adds a punch to this stew. If you can't, plain tofu will work too, just be more generous with the seasoning.

SERVES 4 PEOPLE

2 tablespoons extra virgin
   olive oil
2 shallots, thinly sliced
3 garlic cloves, roughly
   chopped
225g (8oz) smoked tofu,
   broken into 2cm (¾ inch)
   pieces
400ml (14 fl oz/generous
   1½ cups) vegetable stock
2 × 400g (14oz) tins of
   chopped tomatoes
1 × 290g (10¼oz) jar of
   pitted kalamata olives
   in brine
sea salt and freshly ground
   black pepper
toast or grains, to serve

GOES WITH
*Warm Lentil Salad with
Smoked Almonds and
Feta (page 131), Roasted
Aubergine, Tahini Sauce and
Cucumber Salsa on Toast
(page 45), Flourless Chocolate
Cake (page 179)*

Put the oil and shallots into a saucepan along with a pinch of salt and cook over a low heat for 15–20 minutes until the shallots are soft and almost caramelised. Add the garlic and cook for a further 3 minutes, then add the tofu and vegetable stock. Simmer for a few minutes, then add the tomatoes and cook for a further 10 minutes.

Drain the olives, reserving the brine, then halve them. Add the olives to the pan along with 2 tablespoons of the brine. Bring the stew back to a simmer and let everything cook for a few more minutes with the lid on. Check the seasoning and adjust with salt and pepper to taste, then serve with a toast or a grain of your choice.

Leek, Cavolo Nero and White Bean Soup

I first cooked this dish for my family during the second Covid-19 lockdown. It was the middle of winter and I wanted to cook something for everyone that felt nourishing and immune-boosting. This soup really has a kick to it from the ginger and lemon juice, and it completely satisfied our needs at that time. I often cook broths as I love the contrast between textures, sipping on fragrant liquid in between mouthfuls of crunchy veg. This is another recipe that I've shared with my family and that they've all made lots ever since.

SERVES 4 PEOPLE

1 litre (34 fl oz/4¼ cups)
   vegetable stock
2 garlic cloves, crushed
1 thumb-sized piece of fresh
   ginger root, peeled and
   grated
2 bay leaves
2 sprigs of fresh rosemary
3 leeks, trimmed and sliced
   into 5 mm (¼ inch) rounds
juice of 1 lemon
200g (7oz) cavolo nero
   (lacinato kale), stalks
   removed and leaves
   shredded
2 × 400g (14oz) tins of
   cannellini beans, drained
6 tablespoons plain yoghurt
handful of fresh flat-leaf
   parsley, leaves chopped
sea salt and freshly ground
   black pepper

GOES WITH
*Cheese Toastie with Tomato
Chutney (page 34), Baked
Beans on Toast (page 41),
Apple Tarte Tatin (page 176)*

Pour the stock into a large saucepan over a low heat, then add the garlic, ginger, bay leaves and rosemary. Cover and bring to a simmer, then cook for 15–20 minutes until you can really smell the aromatics coming off the liquid.

Once the broth has simmered long enough, add the leeks and the lemon juice and season with salt and pepper. Cover again and cook for a further 10 minutes, then add the cavolo nero and beans, cover again and continue to cook for a final 10 minutes.

When you are ready to serve, ladle the broth into bowls, then finish each bowl with a spoonful of yoghurt and some parsley.

Roasted Tomato, Thyme and Butter Bean Soup

For me, there's nothing quite like tomato soup. I love roasting the tomatoes this way as they release even more sweetness and a delicious, deeper flavour. The addition of butter beans helps this soup feel more substantial, which, as someone with a seemingly neverending appetite, is something I'm always striving for in my cooking. If you would like a thinner soup, just add more vegetable stock.

SERVES 4 PEOPLE

450g (1lb) tomatoes,
   quartered
2 garlic cloves, peeled
   but left whole
4 tablespoons extra virgin
   olive oil, plus extra to serve
1 onion, diced
¼ bunch of fresh thyme,
   leaves picked, plus extra
   to serve
600ml (20 fl oz/2½ cups)
   vegetable stock
2 × 400g (14oz) tins of butter
   (lima) beans, drained
sea salt and freshly ground
   black pepper

GOES WITH
*Cheese Toastie with Tomato
Chutney (page 34), Confit
Garlic (page 149), Herb Butter
(page 147)*

Preheat the oven to 220°C (425°F). Put the tomatoes and garlic into a baking tray (pan) and drizzle with 2 tablespoons of the oil and season with salt and pepper. Roast in the oven for about 20 minutes until they have started to collapse and have coloured a little, shaking the tray or using a spoon to distribute the olive oil occasionally.

Put the remaining oil, the onion, thyme and some salt and pepper into a large heavy-based saucepan and cook over a low heat for 10–15 minutes until the onions are soft.

Once the tomatoes are ready, add them to the onions with all their cooking juices. Add the stock, season again, then let everything cook over a medium heat for 10 minutes.

Remove the pan from the heat and blend the soup with a hand-held blender, then return it to a low heat. Add the beans, then simmer the soup for about 5 minutes until the beans are warmed through.

Serve with a drizzle of olive oil, a crack of black pepper and a few thyme leaves.

White Miso Butter Beans

This recipe is so simple – I love making it for a quick lunch. The creaminess of the miso combined with the comforting beans and warming ginger and garlic make it feel really hearty. You could happily serve this as a side, perhaps leaving out the poached egg. It's also a great dish for when you don't have many ingredients in the refrigerator but you have the staples in your kitchen cupboard.

SERVES 4 PEOPLE

2 tablespoons extra virgin
    olive oil
2 shallots, diced
4 garlic cloves, sliced
3 × 400g (14oz) tins of butter
    (lima) beans, drained
1 thumb-sized piece of
    fresh ginger root, peeled
    and grated
4 tablespoons white miso
    paste dissolved in 400ml
    (14 fl oz/generous 1½ cups)
    hot water
40ml (1¼ fl oz/2¾
    tablespoons) oat milk
1 tablespoon rice vinegar
200g (7oz) spinach leaves
4 medium eggs
1 tablespoon apple
    cider vinegar
juice of ½ lime
½ red chilli, deseeded
    and sliced
¼ bunch of fresh coriander
    (cilantro), leaves roughly
    chopped
sea salt

GOES WITH
*Crispy Kale (page 144),
Sweetcorn, Herb Butter, Chilli
and Pecorino (page 124), New
Potato, Asparagus, Chive and
Egg Salad (page 121)*

Put the oil and shallots into a saucepan with a pinch of salt and cook over a low heat for about 10 minutes until soft, then add the garlic and cook for 2–3 minutes, stirring occasionally to stop it catching.

Add the butter beans, ginger, miso mixture, oat milk and vinegar. Increase the heat to medium and bring to a simmer. Cook for about 10 minutes, then add the spinach and stir it through so that the leaves wilt.

Next, poach the eggs. I poach my eggs one at a time because I find it easier to control the process that way. To poach the eggs, bring a saucepan of water to a simmer over a medium heat, making sure it doesn't boil. If the water starts to boil, turn down the heat slightly. Crack an egg into a cup or small bowl. Add the apple cider vinegar to the water and use the end of a wooden spoon to create a whirlpool in the water. Bring the egg as close to the surface of the water as possible before dropping it in. Cook for 3 minutes, then remove from the water and allow to drain on paper towels before cooking the next egg.

Divide the beans between bowls, squeeze some lime juice over each portion and top each with a poached egg. Finish with the chilli and coriander.

Gazpacho

In the summer, this soup is part of my frequent rotation and I'll often make a big batch and just have it as a snack throughout the week to cool me down or pick me up.

SERVES 4 PEOPLE

1 cucumber, peeled and
  chopped
500g (1lb 2oz) ripe tomatoes,
  chopped
1 head of celery, chopped
1 × 390g (13¾oz) jar of
  sweet piquant red peppers,
  drained
4 tablespoons extra virgin
  olive oil
2 tablespoons sherry vinegar
a pinch of sea salt
a few generous grinds of
  black pepper
¼ bunch of fresh basil leaves,
  plus extra to serve

GOES WITH
Crispy Breadcrumbs (page
155), Warm Lentil Salad
with Smoked Almonds and
Feta (page 131), No-churn
Raspberry Ice Cream
(page 162)

Combine all the ingredients in a food processor and blend until smooth. You might have to do this in batches.

Tip the gazpacho into a large serving bowl and taste to check you are happy with the seasoning. Serve with a couple of basil leaves and an ice cube in the bowl if you need extra cooling down!

Leek and Potato Soup with Cheese on Toast

I love leek and potato soup, which I think is really worth taking time over because you will get incredible flavour from the leeks if they are cooked slowly. We used to have cheese on toast, religiously, every Sunday night growing up, so it's the taste of nostalgia for me. Every time I want to elevate my soup experience, I make a slice of cheese on toast to go with it and it always takes it from good to delicious.

SERVES 4 PEOPLE

2 tablespoons extra virgin olive oil, plus extra to serve
3 leeks, trimmed and sliced into 2cm (¾ inch) rounds
2 bay leaves
3 garlic cloves, sliced
350g (12oz) waxy potatoes, cut into 2cm (¾ inch) chunks
1 litre (34 fl oz/4¼ cups) vegetable stock
3 tablespoons double (heavy) cream, plus extra to serve (optional)
sea salt and freshly ground black pepper
10g (½oz) chives, finely chopped, to serve

FOR THE CHEESE ON TOAST
4 slices of bread
190g (6¾oz) mature Cheddar, grated
10g (½oz) unsalted butter

GOES WITH
Wild Mushroom, Ricotta and Caramelised Onion Tart (page 89), New Potato Frittata with a Fresh Herb Salad (page 90)

Put the oil, leeks, bay leaves and a generous pinch of salt into a large, heavy-based saucepan over a low-medium heat, cover and cook for 10 minutes, stirring occasionally, until the leeks have begun to soften, then remove the lid and cook for a further 10 minutes until they have caramelised slightly. If the leeks start to catch, add a splash of water and reduce the heat.

Once the leeks are cooked, add the garlic and cook for a few minutes until it's translucent, then add the potatoes and stock and season with salt and pepper. Cover, increase the heat to medium and simmer for about 20 minutes until the potatoes have completely softened and you can stick a fork through them. Meanwhile, preheat the oven to 180°C (350°F).

To make the cheese, toast the bread lightly. Top with the butter, evenly distributing it between the four pieces, followed by the Cheddar. Transfer to a lined baking tray and cook for 7–10 minutes, until the cheddar has fully melted.

Once the potatoes are cooked, remove the bay leaves and add the double cream, if using.

Remove from the heat and blend the soup with a hand-held blender until smooth, then divide it between warm bowls and top with the chives, a pinch of salt and pepper and a drizzle of olive oil and some more cream, if you like. Serve each bowl with two slices of cheese on toast, dunked in if you like.

Courgette and Red Pepper Stew
with Buffalo Mozzarella and Almonds

While many soups and stews lend themselves to cold winter days, there are also many that I enjoy making and eating in the summer. I first cooked this in Wales when I had a glut of courgettes (zucchini) from my garden, and I now love making it every summer. Of course, you can skip the buffalo mozzarella and almonds if you want something simple, but if you feel like sprucing things up, definitely give them a go, as the vegetable flavours work so well with the creamy cheese and crunchy nuts.

SERVES 4 PEOPLE

2 tablespoons extra virgin olive oil, plus extra for drizzling
5 garlic cloves, sliced
½ red chilli, deseeded and sliced
20g (¾oz) fresh rosemary, leaves picked and roughly chopped
3 courgettes (zucchini), quartered lengthways and chopped at different angles into 3cm (1¼ inch) pieces
2 red (bell) peppers, chopped into 3cm (1¼ inch) pieces
2 × 400g (14oz) tins of plum tomatoes
1 tablespoon apple cider vinegar
30g (1oz) raw almonds
2 × 125g (4½oz) balls of buffalo mozzarella
10g (½oz) fresh basil, leaves picked
sea salt and freshly ground black pepper

GOES WITH
Simple Slaw (page 143),
Sweetcorn, Herb Butter, Chilli
and Pecorino (page 124),
Peach, Hazelnut and Basil
Galette (page 183)

Preheat the oven to 180°C (350°F).

Put the oil, garlic, chilli and rosemary into a large heavy-based saucepan over a very low heat and cook for about 3 minutes, stirring occasionally to ensure it doesn't catch.

Add the courgettes and peppers along with an extra drizzle of olive oil, season well with salt and pepper and cook over a medium heat for 10 minutes. Add the tomatoes and vinegar and cook for a further 15 minutes.

Meanwhile, spread out the almonds on a baking tray (pan) and toast in the oven for 5–10 minutes until they are golden and smell toasted, checking them regularly. Remove from the oven and set aside to cool. Once cooled, roughly chop.

Remove the stew from the heat and season again, then ladle into warmed shallow bowls and top each one with half a ball of mozzarella with a drizzle of olive oil. Top with a few basil leaves, a scattering of almonds and a pinch of salt and pepper.

Ribollita

This is my version of the beautiful Tuscan soup. I started making this around the same time that I started to make bread because it was a brilliant way to use up any bread going stale. It's a great dish to make in the depths of winter when there is not much fresh produce available, as you can rely on tinned tomatoes to satisfy that need for fresh flavour. The stew starts with a base of slowly cooked onions, celery and carrots, which in Italian cooking is called a soffritto and is the base for many similar dishes – you can adapt this method for almost any broth, soup or stew. Ribollita truly tastes better when it's eaten the next day, as the flavours develop overnight.

SERVES 4 PEOPLE

2 slices of stale sourdough
   bread, cut into 5cm (2 inch)
   chunks (see method)
4 tablespoon extra virgin
   olive oil, plus extra to serve
1 onion, finely diced
3 celery stalks, finely diced
1 carrot, peeled and
   finely diced
2 bay leaves
½ bunch of fresh rosemary,
   leaves picked and finely
   chopped
½ bunch of fresh thyme,
   leaves picked and finely
   chopped
4 garlic cloves, chopped
2 × 400g (14oz) tins of
   plum tomatoes
500ml (17 fl oz/generous
   2 cups) vegetable stock,
   plus more if necessary
200g (7oz) cavolo nero
   (lacinato kale)
sea salt and freshly ground
   black pepper

GOES WITH
*Hugo's Gem Lettuce Caesar
Salad (pae 126), Apple and
Blackberry Pie (page 169)*

Before you make the soup, I suggest that you spread out the chunks of bread on a baking tray (pan) or similar and leave it out on the side to allow it to get as stale as possible. I do this the night before I make it, but a few hours will also work.

Put the oil, vegetables, herbs and a pinch of salt and pepper into a large, heavy-based saucepan over a low heat. Cover and cook for 20–30 minutes, stirring occasionally, until the vegetables are soft and sweet. Not rushing this first step is essential for creating a really flavourful final dish.

Add the garlic and tomatoes and season again, then increase the heat slightly and bring everything to a simmer. Add the stock and cavolo nero and give everything a good stir, then cover and cook for 10 minutes.

Finally, stir in the bread, cover and cook for a final 5 minutes. Check that you are happy with the seasoning, ladle into bowls and drizzle with a little olive oil. Alternatively, leave the soup to cool and warm it up before serving it the next day. I love it topped with freshly grated Parmesan, too.

Smoky Squash Stew with Spinach

I love the smokiness and depth of flavour in this stew. It's rich, hearty and just right for when it's cold outside and I need a bit of extra warmth. When you cook the butternut squash, be careful to season it really generously with sea salt in order to cut through its natural sweetness.

SERVES 4 PEOPLE

1 butternut squash, peeled, deseeded and chopped into 3cm (1¼ inch) chunks
1 tablespoon extra virgin olive oil, plus extra for drizzling
1 red onion, thinly sliced
4 garlic cloves, very finely chopped
½ red chilli, deseeded and sliced
1 tablespoon harissa paste
2 × 400g (14oz) tins of chopped tomatoes
2 tablespoons balsamic vinegar
200g (7oz) spinach leaves
4 tablespoons Greek yoghurt
20g (¾oz) fresh flat-leaf parsley, leaves finely chopped
sea salt and freshly ground black pepper

GOES WITH
Hugo's Gem Lettuce Caesar Salad (page 126), Chocolate Mousse with Whipped Cream (page 172)

Preheat the oven to 180°C (350°F).

Put the squash into a roasting tin, drizzle it with olive oil and sprinkle with a generous pinch of salt and pepper. Roast in the oven for 30 minutes until the squash is soft.

Put the tablespoon of oil and the onion into a large saucepan over a low heat with a pinch of salt and cook for about 10 minutes, stirring frequently, until the onion is very soft and almost caramelised. If the onion starts to catch, add a bit more oil and a dash of water.

Add the garlic and chilli and cook for a few minutes, being careful not to let the garlic burn, then stir in the harissa paste and cook for another couple of minutes.

Add the tomatoes and balsamic vinegar and season generously with salt and pepper. Increase the heat slightly and let everything simmer for about 10 minutes.

Once the squash is ready, add it to the stew, along with the spinach. Mix everything together and simmer for a further 5 minutes.

Divide the stew between bowls, then top each one with a tablespoon of yoghurt, a scattering of parsley and a pinch of salt and pepper.

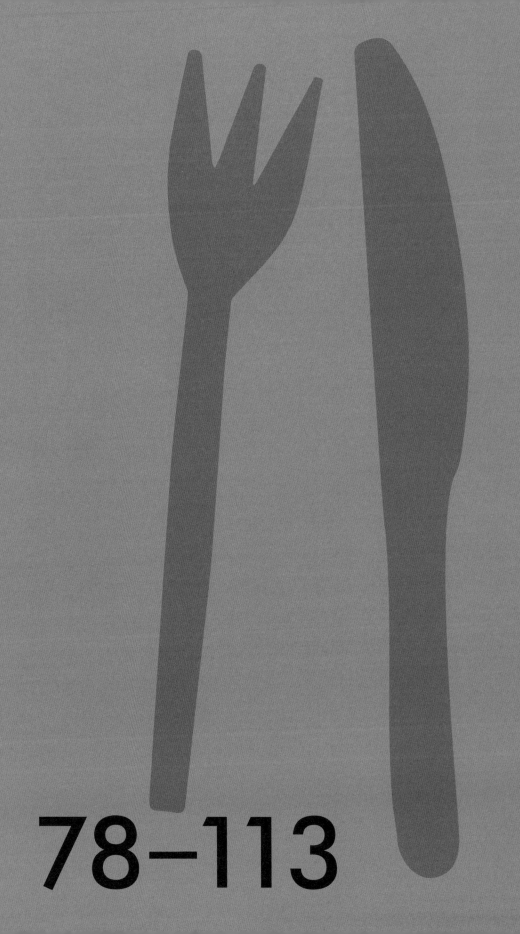

78–113

Mains

The dishes in this chapter are the ones I lean on when I don't want to think too hard about pairing different dishes together, and instead just want to create one satisfying plate of food. They will act as your friend on those solo weeknights when you want to fit something new into your rotation, but don't fancy cooking up multiple things.

While they are slightly more well-dressed than a soup, stew or something on toast, so will happily stand alone, these mains also work well with a side salad, if you feel like it. And, like so many recipes in this book, they can also be elevated to create something you'd be happy to serve to your friends when hosting.

Lentil and Mushroom Bolognese

I love the deep, earthy flavour that the mushrooms bring to this, and the lentils are a good way to build texture. Lentils are such a good staple to have in your kitchen. Not only are they very high in protein, but they also store carbon in the soil as they grow, meaning they help to rebuild the health of our soil. I often eat this with a piece of toast for lunch. You could make it as a starter or snack, too: fill Little Gem or Bibb lettuce leaves with a spoonful and garnish with a pinch of chopped chives. An easy one to make in advance and serve up when your friends arrive.

SERVES 6 PEOPLE

3 tablespoons extra virgin olive oil
1 onion, diced
2 carrots, peeled and diced
3 celery stalks, diced
4–5 dried mushrooms, preferably porcini
190ml (6½ fl oz/generous ¾ cup) cold water
2 garlic cloves, sliced
70g (2½oz) tomato purée (paste)
120g (4¼oz) brown lentils
400–600ml (14 fl oz/generous 1½ cups) vegetable stock
1 × 400g (14oz) tin of chopped tomatoes
200g (7oz) oyster mushrooms (or chestnut/cremini mushrooms), chopped into 1cm (½ inch) pieces
1 tablespoon balsamic vinegar
750g (8¼oz) pasta
sea salt and freshly ground black pepper
grated Parmesan, to serve

GOES WITH
Simple Slaw (page 143), Hugo's Gem Lettuce Caesar Salad (page 126), Flourless Chocolate Cake (page 179)

Put the oil, onion, carrots and celery into a large heavy-based saucepan and season with salt and pepper. Cover and cook for 10–15 minutes until soft.

Meanwhile, put the dried mushrooms into a bowl, cover with the cold water and set aside to soak for about 20 minutes.

Add the garlic and tomato purée to the vegetables, stirring to combine everything, and cook for a few minutes until the garlic softens. Add the lentils, stock and tomatoes. Drain the soaked mushrooms and add the soaking liquid to the pan, reserving the mushrooms. Check the seasoning and add salt and pepper if necessary.

Reduce the heat to a simmer and cook for 20–30 minutes until the lentils are soft but with a slight bite. There will be quite a lot of liquid at first, but don't worry, the lentils will absorb it as they cook.

Once the lentils have been cooking for about 10 minutes, finely chop the soaked mushrooms and add them to the pan along with the oyster mushrooms and balsamic vinegar. Stir the lentils occasionally as they cook to prevent them from sticking to the bottom of the pan.

Once the lentils are cooked and most of the liquid has been absorbed, bring a large saucepan of water to the boil and cook the pasta according to the packet instructions. Divide the pasta between bowls and top with a generous ladle of the Bolognese and a generous grating of parmesan.

Buckwheat Crêpes with Mushrooms and a Fried Egg

These crêpes are one of my life's simplest pleasures. They are so quick and easy and are a lovely supper when you want to change up your rotation. The addition of buckwheat adds a delicious nuttiness and, to me, the combination of toppings is perfect. I'd recommend making all the crêpes first, covering them with a dish towel, and then when you are ready to serve, putting them back in the pan one by one to quickly melt the cheese and add the toppings.

SERVES 4 PEOPLE

8 medium eggs
320ml (11 fl oz/1⅓ cups) whole (full-fat) milk
120g (4¼oz/generous ¾ cup) wholemeal (whole-wheat) buckwheat flour
60g (2oz/½ cup) plain (all-purpose) flour
30g (1oz) unsalted butter, plus extra for frying
200g (7oz) button mushrooms, thinly sliced
2 sprigs of fresh thyme, leaves picked
100g (3½oz) spinach leaves
olive oil, for drizzling
juice of ¼ lemon
50g (1¾oz) Cheddar, grated
sea salt and freshly ground black pepper

GOES WITH
Chocolate Chip and Almond Butter Cookies (page 165)

Break 4 of the eggs into a bowl and whisk with a fork until well combined. Add the milk, both flours and a generous pinch of salt and mix until you have a smooth batter. Set aside to rest while you cook the mushrooms. Melt the butter in a frying pan over a medium heat, add the mushrooms and thyme and season with a sprinkle of salt. Cook for 5–10 minutes until browned.

Put the spinach into a sieve in the sink and pour a kettle full of boiling water over it to cook it. Using the back of a spoon, squeeze out as much water as you can through the sieve. Transfer the spinach to a bowl and dress it with a drizzle of olive oil, the lemon juice and a sprinkle of salt.

Heat a knob of butter in a large non-stick frying pan over a medium heat and when the pan is nice and hot, pour a ladle of the batter into the pan and move it around quickly to make sure it covers the entire base of the pan. Cook the crêpe for 3–5 minutes on one side until it starts to cover, before flipping it over to cook the other side. When the first crêpe is cooked, put it onto a plate and cover it with a clean dish towel to keep it warm. Continue with the remaining batter, melting a knob of butter in the frying pan each time.

When the crêpes are cooked, heat a little more butter in a separate frying pan and fry the remaining 4 eggs over a high heat, then sprinkle with salt and pepper.

While the eggs are cooking, put the crêpes back into the pan one by one and sprinkle over some of the grated Cheddar, leaving them in the pan just long enough for the cheese to melt. Spread some of the spinach and mushrooms in the middle of each crêpe, leaving about 5cm (2 inches) around the edges. Place a fried egg on the middle of each crêpe, then fold over the sides to encase some of the filling. Serve immediately.

Tomato, Aubergine and Mozzarella Lasagne

The Sicilian dish of Pasta alla Norma, with the combination of tomatoes and aubergine (eggplant), is one of my favourites. They are the flavours of summer and complement each other so well. If you're hosting and want to make this recipe easier for yourself, you could make the sauce the night before and then just assemble the lasagne when you want to cook.

SERVES 4 PEOPLE

3 large aubergines (eggplants), chopped into 3cm (1¼ inch) chunks
2 tablespoons extra virgin olive oil, plus extra for drizzling
1 red onion, finely chopped
5 garlic cloves, sliced
2 tablespoons tomato purée (paste)
3 large tomatoes, diced
2 × 400g (14oz) tins of plum tomatoes
40ml (1½ fl oz/3 tablespoons) red wine (or 30ml/ 2 tablespoons red wine vinegar)
1 bunch of fresh basil, leaves and stalks roughly chopped
230g (8¼oz) lasagne sheets
3 × 225g (8oz) balls of buffalo mozzarella, thickly sliced
75g (2½oz) Parmesan, grated (or vegetarian alternative)
sea salt and freshly ground black pepper

GOES WITH
*Sweetcorn, Herb Butter, Chilli and Pecorino (page 124),
Brown Butter Apple Tarte Tatin (page 176)*

Preheat the oven to 180°C (350°F).

Spread the aubergines out on a baking tray (pan), making sure they have plenty of room (use two trays if you need to). Drizzle generously with oil and season with salt and pepper. Roast in the oven for about 30 minutes until very soft, turning them halfway through so that they cook evenly.

Meanwhile, put the 2 tablespoons of oil and the onion into a large saucepan pan along with a generous pinch of salt. Cook over a low heat for 10–15 minutes until soft.

Next, add the garlic and tomato purée and cook for a couple of minutes, then add the diced tomatoes. Increase the heat slightly and cook until the garlic is translucent and the tomatoes have collapsed. Take your time with this – it should take up to 15 minutes for the tomatoes to properly cook down.

Add the tinned tomatoes and red wine, and season everything with salt and pepper. Add the basil, stalks and all, then cover and cook for a further 20 minutes over a medium heat.

When the aubergines are ready, take them out of the oven, but keep the oven on. Add the aubergines to the tomato sauce and cook for 10 more minutes.

To assemble the lasagne, spoon a generous layer of the tomato and aubergine sauce into a 20 x 20cm (8 x 8 inch) baking dish, then cover with a layer of lasagne sheets. Make sure they aren't overlapping or they won't cook properly. Then, add a layer of mozzarella slices and a layer of grated Parmesan. Repeat this whole sequence two more times. This recipe should make enough to do three layers of lasagne, finishing with a layer of pasta followed by mozzarella and Parmesan.

Transfer the dish to the oven and cook for 15 minutes. Increase the heat to 220°C fan (425°F) and cook for 15–25 minutes more, until the top is golden and the pasta is cooked.

Wild Mushroom, Ricotta and Caramelised Onion Tart

Although it's pretty easy to make your own puff pastry, shop-bought is such a good vehicle for piling high with an assortment of delicious toppings, and you can get it in most supermarkets. A tart made like this is also a great snack or starter for when you have friends round and want to make something relatively easy but impressive. Just cut it up into smaller pieces and serve on a nice platter. You always want puff pastry to be cold before cooking it, as this will give you the best puff, so leave it in the refrigerator until just before you need it.

SERVES 6 PEOPLE

5 tablespoons extra virgin olive oil, plus extra for drizzling
1 tablespoon balsamic vinegar
2 red onions, thinly sliced
250g (9oz) ricotta
zest of 1 lemon plus juice of ½
400g (14oz) wild mushrooms of your choice
1 garlic clove, thinly sliced
1 tablespoon white wine or white wine vinegar
plain (all-purpose) flour, for dusting
115g (4oz) cold ready-rolled shop-bought puff pastry
1 medium egg, beaten
sea salt and freshly ground black pepper

GOES WITH
Slow-cooked Ratatouille (page 136), Simple Slaw (page 143), No-churn Raspberry Ice Cream (page 162)

Preheat the oven to 200°C (400°F) and line a baking sheet with baking parchment (use a drizzle of oil under the parchment to secure it).

Put 2 tablespoons of the oil, the balsamic vinegar and onions into a frying pan over a low heat, season with salt and cook for 20–30 minutes until very soft and sweet. The key is to go low and slow, stirring only when you need to stop them burning. If they do start to burn, add about a tablespoon of water and give them a stir.

Meanwhile, combine the ricotta, lemon zest and juice, 1 tablespoon of the oil and a generous pinch of salt and black pepper in a bowl. Stir everything together almost aggressively, so that the ricotta whips a little. Set aside.

Slice the mushrooms into halves or thirds – you want to keep the mushrooms quite big because these will form the centre of the dish, so having some body will look and taste better. Put the remaining 2 tablespoons of oil into a heavy-based frying pan over a medium heat along with the garlic, mushrooms and wine or vinegar. Season with sea salt and pepper, then cook for about 10 minutes until the mushrooms have softened and reduced in size.

Once everything is ready, lightly flour a surface and roll out the pastry slightly, just one roll on all four sides. Slide the pastry onto the prepared baking sheet, then spread the ricotta onto the pastry, leaving a border of about 3cm (1¼ inches) on all sides. Score a border of about 1cm. Top the ricotta with the caramelised onions, followed by the mushrooms. Season with salt and pepper. Brush the beaten egg onto the scored pastry borders, then bake the tart in the oven for 10–15 minutes, or until the pastry is golden brown. Slice and serve immediately.

New Potato Frittata with a Fresh Herb Salad

Frittata has always been a staple when my family are all at home. In the summer, they are filled with courgettes (zucchini), peas and feta. In the winter, the summer vegetables are swapped for squash, onions and sage. Eggs truly are a vehicle for so much deliciousness. I make the salad with parsley, mint and dill but feel free to use whatever soft herbs you have available – basil would be delicious in this too.

SERVES 4 PEOPLE

200g (7oz) new (baby) potatoes, halved
2 tablespoons extra virgin olive oil
1 onion, sliced
3 garlic cloves, thinly sliced
6 medium eggs
1 tablespoon unsalted butter
sea salt and freshly ground black pepper

FOR THE SALAD
½ bunch of fresh flat-leaf parsley
½ bunch of fresh mint
½ bunch of fresh dill
200g (7oz) watercress
1 tablespoon extra virgin olive oil
juice of ½ lemon

GOES WITH
*Squash, Tahini, Crispy Sage and Hazelnuts (page 118),
Roasted Tomato, Thyme and Butter Bean Soup (page 62)*

Preheat the oven to 180°C (350°F).

Start by preparing the herbs for the salad. Pick the parsley and mint leaves from the stalks and put them into a bowl of cold water. Tear the dill fronds into a similar size and add to the water too. Soaking the herbs like this will make them brighter and fresher for the salad. Put the bowl to one side while you prepare everything else.

Put the potatoes into a saucepan of cold, generously salted water. Seasoning the water with salt before you cook the potatoes helps to season the entire potato, not just the outside. Bring to the boil, then reduce the heat to medium and cook the potatoes for 10–15 minutes until a fork easily pierces a potato all the way through, then drain.

Meanwhile, heat the oil in a frying pan over a low heat and add the onions. Season with salt, cover and cook for about 15 minutes until soft, stirring occasionally to ensure they don't catch. Add the garlic and cook for a few minutes until translucent, then remove the pan from the heat and set aside to cool slightly.

Break the eggs into a bowl, season with salt and pepper, and whisk with a fork until fully combined. Once the onions and garlic have cooled, beat them into the eggs.

Heat the butter in a 20cm (8 inch) non-stick ovenproof frying pan over a high heat, add a pinch of salt and then add the potatoes, flesh side down, so that they are covering the bottom of the pan. Cook the potatoes for a couple of minutes, then remove the pan from the heat and add the beaten eggs. Carefully transfer the pan to the oven and cook the frittata for about 10 minutes until they have slightly coloured on the bottom, checking it halfway through.

While the frittata is cooking, make the herb salad. Drain the herbs and lay them out on a dish towel. Pat the herbs dry, then put them into a mixing bowl along with the watercress. Add the oil and lemon juice and a sprinkle of salt. Toss the salad to coat the leaves in the dressing.

Once the frittata is ready, flip it out of the pan and onto a cutting board. Cut it into slices and serve with the herb salad. If there are any leftovers, enjoy them cold!

Cold Noodle Salad with Tahini and Miso Dressing

This recipe is a complete staple in my kitchen. I love the dressing and could drink it from the bowl. If you wanted to serve this warm, you could put the contents of the salad into a frying pan and warm it through, which I like to do in winter, but maybe substitute the vegetables for those that are in season. I love the crunchy cucumber and carrots in summer, though, along with the herbs that really freshen it up. I use avocado very occasionally as a nice indulgence, because of the environmental effects of growing it and shipping it across the world, so when I do, it feels like a real treat. If you're making a meal for eating on the go, this is also a really good one to pack up and take with you.

SERVES 4 PEOPLE

225g (8oz) flat rice noodles
3 carrots, peeled and
  julienned
1 cucumber, peeled and
  julienned
¼ bunch of fresh coriander
  (cilantro), leaves finely
  chopped
¼ bunch of fresh mint, leaves
  finely chopped
2 avocados (optional), sliced
  into 5mm (¼ inch) slices
1 tablespoon sesame seeds
½ red chilli, deseeded and
  thinly sliced
1 lime, quartered

FOR THE DRESSING
4 tablespoons tahini
4 tablespoons cold water,
  plus extra as needed
1 tablespoon sesame oil, plus
  extra for drizzling
2 tablespoons light soy sauce
1 tablespoon apple cider
  vinegar
1 tablespoon white miso paste
3–4cm (1¼–1½ inch) piece
  of fresh ginger root, peeled
  and grated

First, make the dressing. Mix the tahini with the cold water in a small bowl until a smooth paste forms, then add the remaining ingredients and stir vigorously until the dressing is well combined. Add a little more water to loosen the dressing if it is too thick – you want a pourable consistency.

Cook the noodles according to the packet instructions, then rinse them under cold water and transfer them to a large bowl. Drizzle with a little sesame oil and mix, then add the carrots, cucumber and herbs. Toss through the dressing so that it completely coats the noodles and vegetables.

Divide the salad between bowls and top with the avocado slices, if using, a sprinkling of sesame seeds, the sliced chilli and a squeeze of lime.

GOES WITH
Roasted Aubergine, Tahini Sauce and Cucumber Salsa on Toast (page 45), Chocolate Chip and Almond Butter Cookies (page 165)

Leek and Squash Quiche

I've always absolutely loved the process of making pastry, and while it can seem intimidating, I think it's actually quite simple once you've had a few goes. The key is using very cold butter and allowing time between all the stages for the pastry to chill. If you don't want to make the pastry, there is perfectly good shop-bought pastry out there, so go for that instead. The quiche itself is quite indulgent and rich, so I'd suggest having a crisp, fresh salad alongside it to lift it up. I love it with the Simple Slaw on page 143.

SERVES 4 PEOPLE

FOR THE PASTRY

125g (4½oz) very cold unsalted butter, plus extra for greasing
150g (5½oz/scant 1¼ cups) plain (all-purpose) flour, plus extra for dusting
pinch of sea salt
2–3 tablespoons ice-cold water
1 egg, beaten

FOR THE FILLING

½ butternut squash, peeled, halved lengthways, deseeded and cut into 2cm (¾ inch) chunks
2 tablespoons extra virgin olive oil, plus extra for drizzling
30g (1oz) unsalted butter
1 big leek or 2 small, trimmed and thinly sliced (use the green tops – they are full of flavour)
3 garlic cloves, roughly chopped
4 medium eggs
80g (2¾oz) Cheddar, grated
200ml (7 fl oz/scant 1 cup) double (heavy) cream
sea salt and freshly ground black pepper

An hour before you want to make the pastry, cut the cold butter into roughly 1.5cm (½ inch) cubes and then refrigerate it until you are ready.

To make the pastry, put the flour and salt into a food processor, add the butter and pulse until the mixture resembles breadcrumbs – be careful not to overwork it. Add the water 1 tablespoon at a time, pulsing to combine between each addition, until the dough comes together. Turn it out onto a lightly floured surface and shape it into a ball. Flatten the ball into a 3cm (1¼ inch) thick circle and wrap it in cling film (plastic wrap), then chill in the refrigerator for 1 hour.

Grease a 26cm (10 inch) non-stick tart tin (pan) with butter, then remove the chilled pastry from the refrigerator. On a lightly floured surface, flatten the ball into a disc with the heel of your hand, then flour the top lightly and roll it out into a circle that is about 1cm thick. Roll the pastry gently over the rolling pin and lift it over the tin. Carefully drop the pastry in place by rolling it off the rolling pin, making sure that you centralise it. Use your fingertips to gently push the pastry into the edges of the tart tin and around the sides. Leave a little overhang at this stage – you can trim it off once the quiche is cooked. Put the tart tin into the refrigerator to chill for another hour.

Preheat the oven to 200°C (400°F).

Meanwhile, prepare the filling. Put the squash into a roasting tin, drizzle generously with olive oil and season with salt and pepper. Roast for about 30 minutes until the squash is very soft, then remove from the oven and reduce the temperature to 180°C (350°F).

CONTINUED OVERLEAF

GOES WITH
Simple Slaw (page 143),
Slow-cooked Ratatouille (page
136), Poached Pears with
Cream (page 174)

While the squash is roasting, heat the butter in a frying pan over a low heat and cook the green tops of the leeks for about 10 minutes until they are soft and sweet. Add the garlic and the whites of the leeks to the pan along with the 2 tablespoons of oil. Season with salt and pepper and cook for 20–30 minutes until the leeks are very soft. Remove from the heat and add the roasted squash. Mix the vegetables together, then set aside.

Break the eggs into a bowl and whisk until fully combined. Add the Cheddar and cream and give the mixture another whisk. Season with salt and a generous amount of pepper – about 20 grinds.

Remove the pastry case from the refrigerator and line it with baking parchment, making sure it's pushed right to the edges. Pour in baking beans or dried lentils all the way to the top of the tin. Bake in the oven for 15 minutes, then remove the parchment and the beans or lentils and bake for a further 5–10 minutes until golden. Blind baking the pastry will ensure that you don't end up with a soggy bottom on your quiche. Once ready, prick the base with a fork and brush your beaten egg over the pastry to ensure there's no leakage while it's cooking.

Remove the pastry case from the oven and let it cool slightly, then spread the squash and leek mixture evenly over the bottom of the pastry and pour over the egg mixture. Bake in the oven for 20 minutes, or until the eggs are cooked and the quiche is golden on top.

Remove from the oven and cool on a wire rack, then when the tin is cool enough to touch, trim the overhanging pastry, remove the quiche from the tin and transfer it to a serving plate.

Roasted Tomato Rigatoni with Burrata

A very simple version of this, minus the confit garlic and burrata, is my go-to comforting Sunday night meal, so definitely feel free to simplify it to make it suitable for the occasion you're cooking for. The addition of the confit garlic and burrata elevates it if you're having friends round or you want to cook something a little more special.

SERVES 4 PEOPLE

2 × 150g (5½oz) balls
    of burrata
700g (1lb 9oz) cherry
    tomatoes, halved
2 garlic cloves, peeled but
    left whole
extra virgin olive oil,
    for cooking
1 onion, diced
1 tablespoon tomato purée
    (paste)
½ bunch of fresh basil,
    leaves picked
50ml (1¾ fl oz/3½
    tablespoons) double
    (heavy) cream
500g (1lb 2oz) rigatoni
1 head of Confit Garlic
    (page 149)
sea salt and freshly ground
    black pepper

GOES WITH
*Broad Beans and Peas on
Toast (page 38), Flourless
Chocolate Cake (page 179)*

Preheat the oven to 220°C (425°F). Take the burrata out of the refrigerator so it's at room temperature when you're ready to serve.

Put the tomatoes and garlic cloves into a baking tray (pan), drizzle generously with oil and season with salt and pepper. Roast in the oven for 20 minutes.

Meanwhile, put a splash of olive oil, the onion and a pinch of salt into a saucepan over a low-medium heat and cook for about 10 minutes, stirring occasionally, until the onion is soft and translucent. Add the tomato purée, stir to combine and cook for another two minutes.

Shred most of the basil, keeping about eight leaves back for serving. Once the tomatoes are cooked, add them to the onions along with the basil and cream. Season with salt and pepper, then allow to cook for about 10 minutes over a medium heat.

Meanwhile, bring a large saucepan of generously salted water to the boil and cook the rigatoni according to the packet instructions. Drain, reserving about two ladles of the pasta water.

Add the pasta water to the tomato sauce and let it cook for a couple more minutes, then add the rigatoni. Drizzle with a few tablespoons of olive oil and season with a pinch of salt and pepper. Cook over a low heat for just a couple of minutes until the pasta is completely covered with the sauce.

Divide the pasta between shallow bowls and top each bowl with half a ball of burrata. Finish with a few confit garlic cloves, a drizzle of olive oil, salt and pepper and a couple of fresh basil leaves.

Chickpeas in a Puttanesca Sauce

Puttanesca is absolutely one of my favourite pasta sauces – I constantly crave the flavour. I wanted to create a puttanesca-inspired dish that was a little lighter than pasta that I could have for lunch, and this is it. It is well known that puttanesca is made primarily from store-cupboard ingredients, so it's a great one to make when you don't feel like going out to the shops, or if you're coming back home after being away. If you don't follow a vegetarian diet, feel free to add four anchovy fillets, finely chopped and cooked with the garlic, but this dish is still delicious without. If adding anchovies, be careful when adding salt as the anchovies are very salty on their own.

SERVES 4 PEOPLE

2 tablespoons extra virgin olive oil, plus extra to serve
1 onion, diced
3 garlic cloves, very finely chopped
2 × 400g (14oz) tins of plum tomatoes
1 tablespoon red wine vinegar (or red wine if you have a bottle open)
1 × 720g (1lb 9½oz) jar or 2 × 400g (14oz) tins of chickpeas (garbanzos), drained and rinsed
1 × 290g (10¼oz) jar of pitted kalamata olives, drained and quartered
90g (3¼oz) baby capers, drained and roughly chopped
½ bunch of fresh flat-leaf parsley, leaves and tender stalks roughly chopped
sea salt and freshly ground black pepper

GOES WITH
Hugo's Gem Lettuce Caesar Salad (page 126), Simple Slaw (page 143), Blood Orange and Thyme Cake (page 180)

Put the oil and onions into a large saucepan over a low heat, season with salt and pepper, cover and cook for 10–15 minutes until soft, stirring occasionally to ensure they don't catch. Add the garlic and cook for a further 2–3 minutes.

Add the tomatoes, vinegar, chickpeas, olives and capers and season with salt and pepper. Increase the heat and cook for about 15 minutes until the tomatoes have started to reduce.

Serve the chickpea puttanesca topped with parsley and a drizzle of olive oil.

Tofu 'Meatballs' with a Simple Tomato Sauce

These tofu 'meatballs' are such a comforting and satisfying meal – particularly with your favourite pasta (about 500g/1lb 2oz). I love cooking with tofu, as there is an amazing variety of ways in which it can be used. I always recommend using smoked tofu if you can, as it's so flavourful.

SERVES 4 PEOPLE

2 tablespoon extra virgin olive oil
1 onion, diced
4 garlic cloves, diced
2 teaspoons dried oregano
65g (2¼oz) tomato purée (paste)
450g (1lb) smoked tofu
70g (2½oz/1¼ cups) panko breadcrumbs
2 medium eggs, beaten
sea salt and freshly ground black pepper

FOR THE SAUCE

3 tablespoons extra virgin olive oil
3 garlic cloves, diced
2 × 400g (14oz) tins of chopped tomatoes
½ bunch of fresh basil, leaves chopped, plus extra to serve
splash of red wine

GOES WITH

Labneh with Roasted Tomatoes, Thyme and Confit Garlic (page 139), Crispy Kale (page 144), Wild Mushrooms, Butter Beans and Parsley Salsa on Toast (page 32), Chocolate Mousse with Whipped Cream (page 172)

Put the oil, onions and a sprinkle of salt into a saucepan over a low heat, cover and cook for 10–15 minutes until soft. Add the garlic and cook for a few minutes until translucent, then add the oregano and tomato purée, stir and cook for a couple of minutes, then remove from the heat.

Pat the tofu dry with paper towels and cut it into quarters, then put it into a food processor and pulse until it resembles breadcrumbs. Add the tofu to the onion mixture along with the panko breadcrumbs. Stir until well combined.

Once the mixture has cooled a little, add in the eggs slowly, checking to see how wet the mixture is as you go. You may not need all of it.

Use your hands to shape the mixture into 12 balls, placing them on a baking tray (pan) lined with baking parchment as you go. Transfer the tray to the refrigerator and allow the balls to chill and set for at least 1 hour.

Preheat the oven to 180°C (350°F).

While the balls are chilling, make the sauce. Put the oil and garlic into a saucepan over a medium heat and cook for about 3 minutes, stirring frequently so that it doesn't catch. You want it to be soft and sweet, not crispy and bitter. Add the tomatoes, basil and wine, season generously, then let the sauce simmer for 20–30 minutes until the wine has cooked off and the sauce has reduced slightly.

Once chilled, cook the 'meatballs' in the oven for about 20 minutes until they are golden brown, turning them halfway through. Put the meatballs into the pan with the sauce and serve over your favourite pasta shape.

My Mum's Braised Lentils with Salsa Rossa

This recipe has been a family staple for as long as I can remember and has weathered the changes in the family's eating habits from vegan to vegetarian to pescatarian to omnivore and back again! Not only is it deeply warming and delicious on its own, but it also goes with everything: serve it as an accompaniment to sausages, fish, chicken, tofu or even steak. The salsa rossa is a tangy contrast to the smooth lentils. Feel free to stir some wilted spinach through the lentils to add some greens. You could also try serving it as a warm salad with torn mozzarella or soft goat's cheese and Crispy Breadcrumbs (page 155). The recipe for the salsa rossa makes more than you will need for this dish, so I'd suggest keeping it in the refrigerator for 2–3 days and adding it to eggs and toast, eating it with pasta or putting it on anything else you'd like.

4 tablespoons extra virgin
  olive oil, plus extra to serve
knob of unsalted butter
2 onions, finely diced
2 garlic cloves, crushed with
  a pinch of salt
2 carrots, peeled and
  finely diced
2 celery stalks, finely diced
180ml (6 fl oz/¾ cup) red
  wine
500g (1lb 2oz) Puy lentils,
  rinsed
5 bay leaves
few sprigs of fresh thyme
750ml (25 fl oz/3 cups)
  vegetable stock
½ large bunch of fresh flat-
  leaf parsley, leaves and
  stalks chopped

FOR THE SALSA ROSSA
2 tablespoons extra virgin
  olive oil
knob of unsalted butter
1 red onion, finely chopped
2 garlic cloves, crushed with
  a pinch of salt
1 small cinnamon stick
1 teaspoon ancho chilli (hot
  pepper) flakes
2 tablespoons red wine
  vinegar
200g (7oz) medium tomatoes,
  diced
1 × 400g (14oz) tin of good-
  quality plum tomatoes,
  chopped
sea salt and freshly ground
  black pepper

GOES WITH
*Crispy Kale (page 144),
Hugo's Röstis (page 112),
Hugo's Gem Lettuce Caesar
Salad (page 126), Apple and
Blackberry Pie (page 169)*

Start by making the salsa rossa. Heat the olive oil and butter in a saucepan on a low heat. Add the onion, season with a generous pinch of salt and cook gently for about 10 minutes until soft and sweet. Add the garlic and cook for a couple of minutes, then throw in the cinnamon stick and the chilli flakes and cook for a further 5 minutes. Take out the cinnamon stick, add the fresh tomatoes and cook on a medium heat for a few minutes. Once the tomatoes have cooked down a little, add the tinned tomatoes and vinegar. Season with salt and pepper, then cook on a low heat for 15 minutes. Take off the heat and set aside.

Meanwhile, cook the lentils. Heat the olive oil and butter to a large saucepan over a low heat. Add the onions, season with a generous pinch of salt and cook gently for 10 minutes, then add the garlic and cook for another couple of minutes. Add the carrots and celery and cook for about 15 minutes until soft and tender, being careful not to let the vegetables catch and colour.

Add the red wine and cook off the alcohol for a few minutes, then stir in the lentils, bay leaves, thyme and enough stock to cover the lentils.

Bring to a gentle simmer and cook for 30 minutes, or until the lentils are tender but still have a bit of a bite. You may need to add a bit more stock if the lentils are drying out too much. Fish out the woody thyme sprigs, stir in the red wine vinegar and check the seasoning.

Remove the pan from the heat and stir through the chopped parsley, then serve with a drizzle of olive oil and a spoonful of salsa rossa.

Squash and Mascarpone Fusilli

The mascarpone in this pasta makes it feel so decadent and rich. It's perfect for autumn (fall) evenings. Of course, use whichever pasta shape you like, I just love the way the fusilli holds onto the sauce for this dish. I always serve this with Crispy Breadcrumbs (page 155) – they add so much texture, which contrasts with the smooth, creamy sauce.

SERVES 4 PEOPLE

1 butternut squash, quartered lengthways and deseeded
extra virgin olive oil, for cooking
3 garlic cloves, unpeeled
130g (4½oz) mascarpone
1 tablespoon white wine vinegar
500g (1lb 2oz) fusilli pasta
sea salt and freshly ground black pepper

GOES WITH
Crispy Breadcrumbs (page 155), Confit Garlic (page 149), Crispy Kale (page 144), Poached Pears with Cream (page 174)

Preheat the oven to 200°C (400°F).

Place the squash quarters on a baking tray (pan), skin side down. Drizzle generously with oil, season with salt and pepper, then roast in the oven for 30 minutes. After this time, remove the tray from the oven, slice the root ends off the garlic cloves and add them to the tray with an extra drizzle of oil. Return the tray to the oven and roast the squash and garlic for a further 15 minutes until the squash is soft and has coloured a little.

Remove the tray from the oven and set aside to cool slightly. Once the squash is cool enough to handle, scoop out the flesh and pop the garlic cloves out of their skins. Transfer both to a food processor along with the mascarpone and vinegar, and season with salt and pepper. Blend until you have a smooth sauce.

Bring a large saucepan of salted water to the boil and cook the fusilli according to the packet instructions. Drain, reserving about two ladles of the pasta water.

Scrape the sauce into a saucepan, add the pasta water and cook over a medium heat for a couple of minutes, stirring until the water has evaporated slightly and the sauce is hot. Add the cooked fusilli and a drizzle of olive oil, and stir until the pasta is evenly coated in the sauce.

Divide the pasta between bowls and serve straight away.

Miso Aubergines with Sushi Rice and Smashed Cucumber Salad

Miso aubergines (eggplants) have long been a staple in my house, and I regularly rely on this dish when I want something satisfying and fresh. It's really important to give the aubergines plenty of time to cook properly because aubergines will really punish you for rushing them with a chalky and bitter texture and flavour.

SERVES 4 PEOPLE

FOR THE AUBERGINES
2 aubergines (eggplants), halved lengthways
extra virgin olive oil, for drizzling
60g (2oz) unsalted butter
1 tablespoon white miso paste
2 tablespoons white sesame seeds, plus extra for sprinkling
sea salt

FOR THE RICE
280g (10oz) sushi rice
1 tablespoon white sesame seeds

FOR THE CUCUMBER SALAD
2 cucumbers, peeled
20g (¾oz) coriander (cilantro), leaves chopped
1 spring onion (scallion), sliced
4 tablespoons light soy sauce
4 tablespoons Japanese rice vinegar
½ teaspoon clear honey

GOES WITH
Cold Noodle Salad with Tahini and Miso Dressing (page 92),
Flourless Chocolate Cake (page 179)

Preheat the oven to 180°C (350°F).

Using a sharp knife, score the flesh of the aubergines in a criss-cross pattern, cutting right down to the skin. Place them on a baking tray (pan) flesh side up, drizzle with olive oil and sprinkle with a pinch of salt. Roast in the oven for 45 minutes.

Meanwhile, combine the butter and miso paste in a small saucepan over a low heat and cook, stirring, until the butter has melted. Add the white sesame seeds and stir to combine.

After 45 minutes, remove the aubergines from the oven and spread the miso butter evenly over them. Return to the oven and roast for a further 5–10 minutes until the aubergines are completely soft.

While the aubergines are cooking, get the rice and the cucumber salad ready. Cook the sushi rice following the packet instructions, and once ready, stir through a pinch of salt and the sesame seeds.

To make the cucumber salad, bash the whole cucumbers with a rolling pin or something similar, turning them as you go, until they start to fall apart slightly but still hold some shape. Don't worry if the skin splits. Then roughly chop them into chunky, angled pieces. Put the pieces into a bowl along with the coriander and spring onion. Whisk together the soy sauce, rice vinegar and honey, then drizzle the dressing over the cucumbers and stir everything to combine.

Once the aubergines are ready, sprinkle the sesame seeds on top and serve them on a bed of sushi rice with a side of the cucumber salad.

Hugo's Röstis with Green Sauce and Poached Eggs

I wanted to include my husband Hugo's rösti recipe in this book because his entry into my life was largely responsible for why I fell in love with food. He is, and always has been, very natural in the kitchen, and I was immediately inspired by the way he moved around with such ease. We met at university, so in the early days, he'd always make these for me when we were feeling a little fragile from the night before. This recipe will make either four large röstis or eight smaller ones.

SERVES 4 PEOPLE

700g (1lb 9oz) Maris Piper potatoes (or another floury variety)
6 medium eggs
extra virgin rapeseed (canola) oil, for frying
1 tablespoon apple cider vinegar
sea salt

FOR THE GREEN SAUCE
½ bunch of fresh basil, leaves picked
¼ bunch of fresh flat-leaf parsley, leaves picked
¼ bunch of fresh mint, leaves picked
1 tablespoon Greek yoghurt
juice of ¼ lemon
2 tablespoons extra virgin olive oil
freshly ground black pepper

GOES WITH
*Simple Slaw (page 143),
Sweetcorn, Herb Butter,
Chilli and Pecorino (page
124), No-churn Raspberry Ice
Cream (page 162)*

Peel and grate the potatoes, then rinse the grated potato under running water until the water runs clear.

Transfer the rinsed potatoes to a clean dish towel and bring the four corners together. Wring out the liquid from the potatoes over the sink or a bowl until you've got as much out as possible.

Once the potatoes are drained to your satisfaction, transfer them to a bowl. Break 2 of the eggs into a jug (pitcher), whisk them with a fork until combined, then add them to the potatoes and season very generously with salt. Stir until everything is well combined.

Place a dry frying pan over a high heat and leave for a couple of minutes until you can feel the heat coming off the pan when your hand is about 15cm (6 inches) above it. Add a drizzle of oil to the pan, then add a tablespoon of the rösti mixture. Use a spatula to press it down into a flat round shape. Cook for about 3 minutes on each side until the rösti is golden. You can probably make two to three at a time, adding more oil between batches. Transfer the cooked ones to a plate and cover with a clean dish towel to keep warm.

While you're cooking the röstis, make the green sauce. Combine all the ingredients in a food processor and blend until smooth (though some texture is nice too!), seasoning to taste with salt and pepper.

While the the röstis are cooking, poach the remaining 4 eggs. I poach my eggs one at a time because I find it easier to control the process that way. To poach the eggs, bring a saucepan of water to a simmer over a medium heat, making sure it doesn't boil. If the water starts to boil, turn down the heat slightly. Crack an egg into a cup or small bowl. Add the apple cider vinegar to the water and use the end of a wooden spoon to create a whirlpool in the water. Bring the egg as close to the surface of the water as possible before dropping it in. Cook for 3 minutes, then remove from the water and allow to drain on paper towels before cooking the next egg.

Serve the röstis with a tablespoon of green sauce on top followed by a poached egg. Season the egg with salt and pepper.

114–131

Salads

A salad done right is a perfect thing, and this goes back to what I outlined in the introduction about eating seasonally where possible, not only in terms of environmental and personal health, but also in regard to what can satisfy our needs at particular times of year. I love cold, crunchy, fresh salads in the summer and hearty, warm salads like the Warm Lentil Salad with Smoked Almonds and Feta on page 131 in the winter.

Following our guts and eating intuitively according to what we feel like our bodies need is the ultimate goal. Salads can be so versatile. I hope that this chapter will invite you to get confident and creative with your salads, thinking of them as a key element needed to lift the entire meal. Look back to the soups and stews and think about how you can work towards building blocks of flavour in salads in the same way that we did for those recipes. This will result in a perfectly well-rounded and delicious plate of food. Many of these salads could stand alone as full meals in themselves, perfect for a weekday lunch. But remember that most meals are made infinitely better with a condiment or two and a slice of toast generously slathered with salty butter.

Squash, Tahini, Crispy Sage and Hazelnuts

I first developed this dish for a supper club and have made it frequently at home since. It really is the taste of autumn (fall). It's important to not shy away from seasoning the squash generously, since it is very sweet by nature. The tahini sauce in this dish is the same one used for the Roasted Aubergine, Tahini Sauce and Cucumber Salsa on Toast on page 45. It's such a versatile sauce, and this is an example of how you can chop and change elements of certain dishes to keep them feeling creative and new. The crispy sage is very adaptable and goes well with fried eggs.

SERVES 4 PEOPLE

1 butternut squash, peeled, halved lengthways, deseeded and cut into 1.5cm (½ inch) slices
120ml (4 fl oz/½ cup) extra virgin olive oil
55g (2oz/generous ⅓ cup) blanched hazelnuts
½ bunch of fresh sage leaves, picked
2 × quantity Tahini Sauce (page 45)
sea salt and freshly ground black pepper

GOES WITH
Smoked Tofu in Tomato and Olive Sauce (page 58), Wild Mushroom, Ricotta and Caramelised Onion Tart (page 89), Poached Pears with Cream (page 174)

Preheat the oven to 180°C (350°F).

Place the squash on a baking tray (pan), drizzle generously with olive oil and season with salt and pepper. Roast in the oven for 30 minutes.

Meanwhile, prepare the hazelnuts and sage. Put the hazelnuts onto a baking tray and toast them in the oven for 5 minutes, keeping a close eye on them. Remove from the oven and allow to cool, then roughly chop them into quarters.

Heat 100ml (4 fl oz) of the olive oil in a small frying pan over a high heat. Depending on the size of your pan you may need to add more, because if the sage leaves aren't covered in oil, they'll go brown rather than stay green. When the oil is hot, turn the heat to medium, add the sage leaves and sprinkle them with salt. Keep a very close eye on them and move them around the pan regularly using a pair of tongs. It should take a few minutes for them to turn crispy – once they have turned dark green, you will know they are ready. Remove the leaves from the oil with tongs and lay them on paper towels to drain.

Spoon the tahini sauce evenly across a large serving plate and arrange the squash slices on top. Drizzle with the remaining oil, season with salt and pepper and finish with the sage leaves and toasted hazelnuts sprinkled evenly across the dish.

New Potato, Asparagus, Chive and Egg Salad

When I lived in Wales, I lived a mile away from a field of asparagus and so had the complete pleasure of having a constant supply of it in my kitchen and would often make this salad often with new season potatoes. Asparagus is a perennial vegetable to grows in the same field year after year. When you see how much of a commitment it is, how it grows and how time-consuming it is to harvest, you really appreciate what a special vegetable it is. You can keep the skin on the potatoes, but I find that more flavour is absorbed by them when they're peeled. This salad really is the epitome of spring and embodies the excitement of the season ahead.

SERVES 4 PEOPLE

750g (1 lb 10oz) new (baby) potatoes, halved

400g (14oz) asparagus, woody ends snapped off and halved lengthways

4 medium eggs

½ teaspoon Dijon mustard

juice of ½ lemon

1 tablespoon good-quality mayonnaise

4 tablespoons extra virgin olive oil

½ bunch of fresh chives, finely chopped

¼ bunch of fresh mint, leaves picked and finely chopped

sea salt and freshly ground black pepper

GOES WITH

Warm Lentil Salad with Smoked Almonds and Feta (page 131), Whipped Ricotta and Asparagus Bruschetta (page 37), Cannellini Bean and Parsley Dip (page 156)

Half-fill a saucepan with very generously salted water: it should taste like seawater. This will ensure that the potatoes are seasoned all the way through rather than just on the outside. Add the potatoes to the pan, bring the water to the boil and cook the potatoes for 12–15 minutes until they can be easily pierced with a fork. Be careful they don't overcook and go fluffy. Drain the potatoes and set aside.

Bring the pan of water back to the boil, add the asparagus and cook for 2–3 minutes until tender but with some bite, then drain and run under cold water to stop them cooking any further.

Bring another small saucepan of water to the boil and add the eggs, using a ladle or a large spoon. Cook for 7 minutes, then carefully remove the eggs (keeping the pan of water) and put them into a bowl of cold water. When they are cool enough to handle, peel and halve them and set aside.

Whisk together the mustard and lemon juice in a small bowl, then stir in the mayonnaise and finally whisk in the oil. Season with salt and a generous amount of pepper.

Combine everything in a large bowl along with the herbs and gently toss the dressing through the salad.

Chicory, Apple, Celery and Blue Cheese Salad

Although I tend to lean towards cooking and eating warm salads in the winter, I love making the most of the delicious vegetables and fruit that are still in season at that time of year. I especially think that fresh, crunchy salads go well with a lot of the heavier, richer dishes that we tend to cook over winter, such as thick soups, creamy beans or vegetarian meatballs. They complement and lift one another up, which I often feel like I need in winter. I know that blue cheese can be a bit divisive, so feel free to swap it for a soft, creamy goat's cheese.

SERVES 4 PEOPLE

30g (1oz/scant ⅓ cup) walnut
    halves
2 green apples, quartered,
    cored and thinly sliced
4 celery stalks, thinly sliced
2 heads of chicory (Belgian
    endive), leaves separated
1 tablespoon apple cider
    vinegar
1 teaspoon Dijon mustard
½ teaspoon clear honey
1 tablespoon extra virgin
    olive oil
75g (2¾oz) mild blue cheese,
    roughly chopped
sea salt and freshly ground
    black pepper

GOES WITH
*Cannellini Bean and Parsley
Dip (page 156), My Mum's
Braised Lentils with Salsa
Rossa (page 106), Warm Lentil
Salad with Smoked Almonds
and Feta (page 131), Tomato
Chutney (page 154)*

Preheat the oven to 180°C (350°F).

Spread the walnuts out on a baking tray (pan) and toast them in the oven for 5 minutes until golden. Shake the baking tray after a couple of minutes and keep a close eye on the walnuts to ensure they don't burn. Remove from the oven and allow to cool, then break them into smaller pieces.

Put the apples, celery, chicory and walnut pieces into a large bowl.

To make the dressing, simply whisk together the vinegar, mustard, honey and oil in a small bowl and season with a pinch of salt and a generous grinding of pepper.

Pour the dressing onto the salad and give everything a good mix to coat. Gently toss through the blue cheese, making sure it is evenly distributed.

Crunchy Bean and Summer Veg Salad

Whenever there's a heatwave in the UK, all I crave is fresh vegetables to cool me down. As you will know by now, I really like cooking and eating according to the season, and that also means day to day, depending on what it's like outside. On some days in the summer, I just want something quick, cold and crunchy, and this salad is the perfect thing for that. I highly recommend using high-quality beans, jarred if possible, as it'll really take the salad up a level.

SERVES 6 PEOPLE

1 × 720g (1lb 9½oz) jar or
  2 × 400g (14oz) tins of
  cannellini beans, drained
  and rinsed
1 × 720g (1lb 9½oz) jar or
  2 × 400g (14oz) tins of
  kidney beans, drained
  and rinsed
1 cucumber, peeled, quartered
  lengthways and chopped
  into 1cm (½ inch) pieces
1 red pepper, chopped into
  1cm (½ inch) pieces
225g (8oz) tomatoes,
  chopped into 1cm (½ inch)
  pieces
3 celery stalks, chopped into
  1cm (½ inch) pieces
3 tablespoons balsamic
  vinegar
2 tablespoons sherry vinegar
2 banana shallots, finely diced
4 tablespoons extra virgin
  olive oil
sea salt and freshly ground
  black pepper

GOES WITH
*Cannellini Bean and Parsley
Dip (page 156), Cheese
Toastie with Tomato Chutney
(page 34), Rosemary and
Garlic Chips (page 152)*

Put the beans and all the vegetables except the shallots into a bowl and mix gently.

To make the dressing, combine the vinegars, shallots and oil with a pinch of salt and a generous grind of pepper in a bowl and whisk until combined. Taste the dressing and adjust the seasoning if needed.

Toss the dressing through the salad and refrigerate for about 30 minutes. This allows the beans and vegetables to absorb the dressing before you serve the salad nice and chilled. However, if you are in a rush, you can of course enjoy the salad straight away.

Sweetcorn, Herb Butter, Chilli and Pecorino

I love corn on the cob, and there are so many ways to take it from a simple side into something exciting, beautiful and significant. I used to make this straight on the open fire in Wales, but it's easy to create it in your kitchen at home too. This dish demonstrates that when you use good-quality, seasonal ingredients, you don't need to tamper with them too much. Enjoy it on a warm, late-summer evening. If you don't want to make the herb butter to serve with this, you could easily make it with normal unsalted butter too.

SERVES 4 PEOPLE

4 corn cobs
30g (1oz) Herb Butter (page 147) or unsalted butter
40g pecorino, grated
½ red chilli, sliced (optional)
¼ bunch of fresh coriander, leaves chopped
juice of ½ lime
sea salt and freshly ground black pepper

GOES WITH
Hugo's Röstis with Green Sauce and Poached Eggs (page 112), Lentil and Mushroom Bolognese (page 82), Wild Mushroom, Ricotta and Caramelised Onion Tart (page 89), Simple Slaw (page 143), Crunchy Bean and Summer Veg Salad (page 123)

Bring a large saucepan of salted water to the boil and cook the corn for 3–5 minutes until it has turned bright yellow. How long the corn takes will depend on how fresh it is, so keep an eye on it after 3 minutes.

Drain the water from the saucepan and add the herb butter. Place the lid on the saucepan, leave the butter to melt for a few minutes, then toss to coat thoroughly.

As soon as the corn is ready, remove it from the pan and put it onto a plate. Season each cob with salt and pepper and then top with the pecorino, chilli and parsley. Squeeze the lime juice over and serve immediately.

Hugo's Gem Lettuce Caesar Salad

My husband Hugo is the master of dressings and he's been making this one for me for years. I wanted to include this recipe in the book because I've borrowed it for supper clubs – I think this salad is such a good starter or side. It's light but indulgent, which settles rumbling stomachs in just the right way. It's so simple and perfect as it is, but please feel free to add other vegetables to it if you're choosing to serve it as a meal in itself. You could also add boiled eggs to make it more substantial. If you're not vegetarian, I'd recommend adding a couple of anchovy fillets to the dressing.

SERVES 4 PEOPLE

3 Little Gem lettuces,
 leaves separated
20g (¾oz) Parmesan (or
 vegetarian alternative),
 grated
½ × quantity Crispy
 Breadcrumbs (page 155)

FOR THE DRESSING
1 garlic clove, crushed with a
 pinch of salt
2 medium egg yolks
1 tablespoon Dijon mustard
1 teaspoon Worcestershire
 sauce
1 tablespoon white wine
 vinegar
150ml (5 fl oz/⅔cup)
 extra virgin olive oil
30g (1oz) Parmesan (or
 vegetarian alternative),
 grated
juice of ½ lime
sea salt and freshly ground
 black pepper

GOES WITH
*Rosemary and Garlic
Chips (page 152), Crispy
Breadcrumbs (page 155),
Lentil and Mushroom
Bolognese (page 82),
Meringue Tower (page 166)*

First, make the dressing. I recommend using a food processor for this dressing, as it makes it easier, but you can also make it using a whisk.

Put the garlic, egg yolks, mustard, Worcestershire sauce and vinegar into a food processor and blend until smooth. With the motor running, slowly trickle in the oil until emulsified. If you are making the dressing by hand, whisk the ingredients together, adding a spoonful of oil at a time and whisking until it's fully incorporated before adding more. Or you could ask someone to help you drizzle in the oil while you whisk.

Once all the oil is incorporated, add the Parmesan and lime juice and season with a generous pinch of salt and about ten grinds of pepper. Add 2 tablespoons of cold water to the dressing, or enough so that it is the consistency of double cream.

Arrange the lettuce leaves on a large plate. Drizzle generously with the dressing and finish with the grated Parmesan and crispy breadcrumbs.

Warm Lentil Salad with Smoked Almonds and Feta

This is a substantial salad that is perfect for any time of year, but I love to eat it on cold winter days. The lentils are cooked using my mum's recipe on page 106, and they act as the perfect foundation for smoked almonds, feta and kale, which transform it into a fresh and different dish that can be served warm or at room temperature.

SERVES 4 PEOPLE

300g (10½oz) kale,
  stalks removed
250g (9oz) braised lentils
  (page 106)
200g (8oz) salad leaves
100g (3½oz) feta
handful of parsley leaves,
  roughly chopped
50g (1¾oz) smoked almonds
  (or regular toasted
  almonds), roughly chopped

FOR THE DRESSING
1 teaspoon Dijon mustard
1 tablespoon white
  wine vinegar
½ teaspoon clear honey
3 tablespoons extra virgin
  olive oil
sea salt and freshly ground
  black pepper

GOES WITH
*Chicory, Apple, Celery and
Blue Cheese Salad (page
122), Leeks with Roasted
Garlic and Walnut Sauce
(page 140), Tomatoes on
Toast (page 28), Brown Butter
Apple Tarte Tatin (page 176)*

Bring a large saucepan of salted water to the boil and blanch the kale leaves for 2 minutes, then drain and transfer to a bowl of ice-cold water.

Make the dressing by whisking together the mustard and vinegar in a bowl until smooth, then adding the honey and finally drizzling in the olive oil. Season with salt and pepper and taste the dressing to check that you're happy with it.

Put the lentils, kale, salad leaves, feta and parsley into a bowl, then add the dressing and mix it through the salad. Heap a generous portion onto each plate and finish with the smoked almonds.

132–157

Sides and Condiments

In this book, I suggest pairing different dishes together as a way to elevate everyday meals or meals for friends. Condiments and sides can act as the perfect bridge between these dishes, rounding things off in just the right way.

Condiments are little spoonfuls of joy that can lift up any dish or meal and make every mouthful more sensational. The sides in this section are some of my favourite in the book and many of them can be so easily used alongside one another to make up a full supper, or even by themselves with a piece of toast for lunch.

I really believe that food should be enjoyed to its fullest capacity every day of our lives, and adding texture, extra flavour or colour to a plate of food will do wonders for this. The condiments and sides in this section can be made in advance and stored in an airtight container for two to three days. They are an ideal way to treat yourself with kindness throughout the week, adding little sprinklings on top of everything you cook. I think most salads are made better with the addition of Crispy Breadcrumbs (page 155) and indeed most pasta sauces with the addition of Confit Garlic (page 149). Prepare to pile your plate even higher.

Slow-cooked Ratatouille

Ratatouille is the taste of summer. It's perfect for warm evenings or weekends when you have lots of produce in the refrigerator to use up. On holiday in France, my mum used to make a huge pot of this over the fire and we'd have it with sausages that had also been cooked over the fire and salad from the garden. Afterwards, we'd toast marshmallows, which later were replaced with wine and cheese. We'd sit outside for hours until it was dark, then watch for shooting stars until we couldn't keep our eyes open. Every time I make this, it reminds me of those special evenings.

SERVES 4 PEOPLE

2 aubergines (eggplants),
     roughly chopped
3 courgettes (zucchini),
     roughly chopped
120ml (4 fl oz/ ½ cup)
     extra virgin olive oil
1 onion, diced
4 garlic cloves, roughly
     chopped
4 tomatoes, diced
2 × 400g (14oz) tins of
     chopped tomatoes
small bunch of fresh basil,
     leaves shredded
1–2 tablespoons red
     wine vinegar
200g (7oz) chestnut (cremini)
     mushrooms, halved
sea salt and freshly ground
     black pepper

GOES WITH
*Sauerkraut (page 150),
Sweetcorn, Herb Butter, Chilli
and Pecorino (page 124),
Rosemary and Garlic Chips
(page 152), Simple Slaw
(page 143), Peach, Hazelnut
and Basil Galette (page 183)*

Preheat the oven to 200°C (400°F).

Put the aubergines and courgettes onto a baking tray (pan), drizzle with 4 tablespoons of the olive oil, season with salt and pepper and roast in the oven for about 40 minutes until the vegetables are cooked and slightly charred. Turn them in the tray a couple of times during the cooking so that they cook evenly and don't burn.

Put the remaining oil and the onion into a large heavy-based saucepan along with a pinch of salt. Cook over a low heat for about 10 minutes until the onion is soft, stirring occasionally to ensure it doesn't catch. Add the garlic and cook for a few more minutes, watching so it doesn't burn.

Add the diced tomatoes to the pan and cook, stirring regularly, for about 10 minutes, then add the tinned tomatoes, basil and red wine vinegar. Check the seasoning, add the mushrooms and let everything cook for a further 20 minutes.

Once the aubergines and courgettes are cooked, add them to the sauce. Cover and let everything cook slowly for as long as you like until it's rich and reduced. Try to leave it for at least 20 minutes, but longer if you can.

Labneh with Roasted Tomatoes, Thyme and Confit Garlic

This is inspired by something that I cooked with my great friend and mentor, Damian Clisby. We have cooked together a lot and I always learn so much from him. I've made iterations of this dish for supper clubs many times since and it always goes down a treat with bread to mop up the labneh with. Labneh is a Middle Eastern cream cheese made by hanging yoghurt in muslin (cheesecloth) overnight or for a few hours. It is so simple to make but feels exciting. The labneh in this recipe works well topped with many things, so feel free to make it as an accompaniment to different creations, too. I also love it with roasted carrots or squash in autumn (fall), or with asparagus in spring.

SERVES 4 AS A SIDE

FOR THE LABNEH
700g (1lb 9oz) Greek yoghurt
generous pinch of sea salt,
    plus extra as needed
3 tablespoons extra virgin
    olive oil

FOR THE ROASTED TOMATOES
400g (14oz) tomatoes of
    mixed size and shape
2 garlic cloves, peeled
5 sprigs of fresh thyme
3 tablespoons extra virgin
    olive oil
sea salt and freshly ground
    black pepper

TO SERVE
Confit Garlic (page 149)
3–4 sprigs of fresh thyme,
    leaves picked

GOES WITH
*Roasted Aubergine, Tahini
Sauce and Cucumber Salsa on
Toast (page 45), Warm Lentil
Salad with Smoked Almonds
and Feta (page 131), Meringue
Tower (page 166)*

You will need to make the labneh at least 8 hours before you want to serve this dish, or ideally the night before.

Put the yoghurt into a bowl and add the salt, then spoon the yoghurt into the middle of a large piece of muslin (cheesecloth). Bring the corners together, then grasp the muslin just above the yoghurt and tie a length of string around it. Hang the labneh over a bowl or the sink and set aside for at least 8 hours, or overnight. The whey (liquid) will separate from the yoghurt and drip through the muslin and you will be left with a fresh cream cheese.

Once the labneh is ready, spoon it into a bowl and season it again, then add the olive oil and mix everything together. Taste it to check whether it needs more seasoning.

To roast the tomatoes, preheat the oven to 200°C (400°F). Put the whole tomatoes into a baking tray (pan) with the garlic cloves, thyme sprigs, olive oil and salt and pepper. Give the tray a shake to mix everything together, then roast the tomatoes in the oven for about 15–25 minutes, depending on their size, until they have started to slightly blister and split. (Alternatively, the tomatoes can be cooked in a sieve over an open fire, which is how Damian first showed me how to make this.) Once cooked, remove the tomatoes from the oven and set aside to cool for a few minutes, as you don't want to put them onto the labneh when they are very hot.

Once you are ready to serve, spread a few spoonfuls of labneh onto a large plate. Top with the roasted tomatoes, then drizzle with the delicious juices. Add 3–4 whole confit garlic cloves on top and a generous amount of the garlic oil. Sprinkle with the thyme and and finish with a pinch of salt and pepper.

Leeks with Roasted Garlic and Walnut Sauce

This dish is inspired by the beautiful French classic, leeks vinaigrette. I absolutely love leeks when they are cooked this way, and this method adds a new dimension to the original. The whole dish can be made a few hours in advance, or even the day before you serve it, as it's best eaten at room temperature rather than piping hot, which means it lends itself perfectly to hosting. It would also be delicious served on toast for a solo lunch.

SERVES 4 PEOPLE

2 bay leaves
1 tablespoon peppercorns
2 leeks
8 garlic cloves, unpeeled
extra virgin olive oil, for
    drizzling
40g (1½oz) walnut halves
4 tablespoons Greek yoghurt
1 tablespoon white wine
    vinegar
sea salt and freshly ground
    black pepper

GOES WITH
*Squash, Tahini, Crispy Sage
and Hazelnuts (page 118),
Crispy Breadcrumbs (page
155), Confit Garlic (page
149), Wild Mushroom, Ricotta
and Caramelised Onion Tart
(page 89), Flourless Chocolate
Cake (page 179)*

Preheat the oven to 180°C (350°F).

Fill a heavy-based saucepan with salted water and add the bay leaves and peppercorns.

Trim the roots and green tops from the leeks and remove the first layer of leaves, then wash off any grit. Slice the leeks in half lengthways, then put them into a pan of water with the aromatics. Place the saucepan over a medium heat, bring to a simmer and then cook for 7–10 minutes until the leeks are soft.

Drain the leeks and leave them in the colander while you prepare the sauce, so that as much water as possible drains out.

Put the garlic cloves onto a small baking tray (pan) and drizzle with enough olive oil to submerge the garlic, then roast them in the oven for 15–20 minutes, or until the garlic is very soft. Remove the tray from the oven and add the walnuts, then return to the oven to roast for a further 5 minutes. Remove and allow to cool.

When the garlic is cool enough to handle, pop the cloves out of their skins and transfer them to a food processor along with the toasted walnuts, yoghurt and white wine vinegar. Season with salt and pepper, then blend until smooth.

To serve, spread the sauce over a large serving plate and arrange the leeks neatly on top. Season with salt and pepper.

Simple Slaw

This slaw is the perfect side dish for the summer months when there is an abundance of vegetables available and all you desire is crisp vegetables. I actually like to make my slaw a few hours in advance, so that the vegetables soften and really absorb the dressing, but it's also great made at the last minute, so it depends what you have time for. I usually serve this alongside a big lunch of cheese, bread, pickles and other picky dishes – perfect summer eating. If you have a mandoline, you can use that to slice everything except the herbs, being careful of your fingers in the process. If you don't have a mandoline, just use a sharp knife and take your time to slice everything as thinly as possible.

SERVES 6 AS A SIDE

½ white cabbage,
   thinly sliced
½ red cabbage, thinly sliced
1 red (bell) pepper,
   thinly sliced
½ bunch of radishes
   (about 4–5), thinly sliced
1 cucumber, peeled and
   thinly sliced
½ bunch of fresh dill,
   fronds thinly sliced
½ bunch of fresh mint,
   leaves thinly sliced
4 tablespoons extra virgin
   olive oil
juice of 2 lemons
generous pinch of sea salt

GOES WITH
*Smoky Squash Stew with
Spinach (page 76), My
Mum's Braised Lentils with
Salsa Rossa (page 106),
Caramelised Leeks, Toasted
Walnuts and Fried Eggs on
Toast (page 42)*

Add all of the sliced vegetables to a big mixing bowl, then add all the chopped herbs, olive oil, lemon juice and salt.

Using two big spoons, give the slaw a really good mix so that the dressing is fully incorporated, and then serve. Add more lemon juice if you think it necessary once you've tasted the salad.

Crispy Kale

This is so simple but I love it because of that. Crispy kale can be the perfect snack on its own, or else it's such a good addition to any of the mains in this book. Try putting it on top of a stew to give it a crunch. I've been making this for years and it never fails me.

SERVES 4 PEOPLE

300g (10½oz) curly kale,
   stalks removed and leaves
   roughly chopped
juice of ¼ lemon
2 tablespoons extra virgin
   olive oil
a generous pinch of sea salt
1 teaspoon chilli (hot pepper)
   flakes (optional)

GOES WITH
*Slow-cooked Ratatouille (page
136), Tofu 'Meatballs' with a
Simple Tomato Sauce (page
104), Squash and Mascarpone
Fusilli (page 109)*

Preheat the oven to 210°C (410°F).

Combine all the ingredients in a bowl and mix to combine. Once the kale is well coated, evenly distribute it onto a baking tray (pan), making sure it's spread out as it won't crisp up if it's overlapping. Use two baking trays if necessary. Roast in the oven for about 10 minutes, or until it's crispy.

Enjoy as a snack or alongside your favourite stew.

Pickled Summer Vegetables

Pickling vegetables in summer reminds me of growing my own vegetables. In the late summer, I would often have an excess of vegetables that needed using up, and pickling is the perfect way to do so. Back in the days before so many types of fresh vegetables were accessible all year round, pickling was the way that summer produce could sustain us all through winter. Snacking on these pickles as they are is so satisfying, but I also love them with a plate of cheese and crackers.

MAKES 1 × 1 LITRE (34 FL OZ) JAR

½ cauliflower, cut into florets, stalks chopped
1 cucumber, quartered lengthways, then cut into 2cm (¾ inch) chunks
200 g (7 oz) cherry tomatoes
160 ml (5½ fl oz/⅔ cup) apple cider vinegar
800 ml (27 fl oz/3⅓ cups) water
40g (1½oz/scant ¼ cup) caster (superfine) sugar
1 tablespoon sea salt

GOES WITH
Cannellini Bean and Parsley Dip (page 156), Caramelised Leeks, Toasted Walnuts and Fried Eggs on Toast (page 42), Burnt Courgette, Basil and Cannellini Bean Stew (page 54)

Put the vegetables into a bowl and tumble them with your hands so that they mix together.

Put the apple cider vinegar, water, sugar and salt into a saucepan and bring to a simmer over a medium heat. Once the sugar and salt have dissolved, remove the pan from the heat. Let the pickling liquid cool completely.

Fill a sterilised 1 litre (34 fl oz) Kilner (Mason) jar (page 150) with the mixed vegetables, then pour over the cooled pickling liquid, adding more water if necessary to make sure that the vegetables are completely covered.

Close the jar and leave it in a cool place in your kitchen, out of direct sunlight. Leave it to pickle for at least 3 days, preferably 5, depending on how deep you like the pickle flavour to be and how warm it is. If it's warmer, the vegetables will need less time, if it's colder, they'll need more. Once you've opened the jar, store the pickles in the refrigerator and eat within a month.

Herb Butter

I often make this to serve with fresh bread if I don't have the time or energy to make a proper starter when I'm having people over for dinner. It looks and tastes impressive and is the perfect way to elevate something simple. I have suggested parsley and chives, but you can really make this with any fresh herbs you'd like. Make sure the butter is at room temperature for a few hours before you want to make this.

MAKES 250G (9OZ)

250g (9oz) unsalted butter
¼ bunch of fresh chives,
   finely chopped
¼ bunch of fresh parsley,
   leaves finely chopped
a generous sprinkle of
   sea salt
fresh bread, to serve

GOES WITH
*My Mum's Braised Lentils
with Salsa Rossa (page 106),
Crunchy Bean and Summer
Veg Salad (page 123)*

Put the butter, herbs and sea salt into a bowl and use a wooden spoon to mix everything together thoroughly. You could also do this in a food processor to make life easier.

Cut out an A3-sized piece of baking parchment and spread the butter along it in a rough line. The aim is to create a sausage shape with the butter, so fold and tuck the paper in on the butter, moving slowly and carefully to make sure the shape is a tight roll.

Put the butter in the refrigerator, then, when you are ready to serve, remove it from the baking parchment, cut it into discs and arrange it on a butter dish. Top with an extra sprinkle of sea salt and serve with fresh bread.

Confit Garlic

I'm sure you've seen confit garlic on a menu somewhere and thought it looks exciting. It is, and it is also so easy to make. If you're thinking of hosting a supper club or just having friends over for dinner, this is the ideal way to elevate a dish like my Roasted Tomato Rigatoni (page 100). It does use a lot of olive oil, so make sure to save the delicious garlic-infused oil and use it for something else. Just store it in a clean glass bottle or jar and drizzle it on salads, use it to cook with, or just be indulgent and mop it up with bread.

MAKES 1 SMALL JAR

1 head of garlic, cloves
    peeled and trimmed
180ml (6 fl oz/ ¾ cup)
    extra virgin olive oil
pinch of sea salt

GOES WITH
*Squash and Mascarpone
Fusilli (page 109), Warm Lentil
Salad with Smoked Almonds
and Feta (page 131)*

Put the garlic cloves into a small saucepan and add the olive oil and salt. Cook very gently over a low heat until the oil starts to bubble. Remove the pan from the heat and allow to cool slightly, then return the pan to the heat. Repeat this process of heating and cooling a few times until the garlic cloves are very soft and some have turned golden. The garlic will burn easily, so keep a close eye on it. The whole process should take about 20 minutes.

When the garlic is ready, either serve it immediately or store it in a clean jar in its oil for a few days and use sparingly.

Sauerkraut

My palate longs for salty and sour things. I add pickles to pretty much every meal – breakfast, lunch or supper! Given this habit, it can become expensive to buy pickles, so making them is definitely wise and really doesn't take long. I love serving pickles as a snack to begin my supper clubs; they always look pretty and guests love them. If you get into a good routine, you can have a jar of sauerkraut constantly pickling in your kitchen so you know you always have it. You can easily swap out the white cabbage for a red one, it works just as well. Always make your pickles in glass jars, if you can, making sure you sterilise the jar beforehand by pouring a kettle of boiling water over it, then drying it with a clean dish towel.

MAKES 1 × 500ML (17OZ) JAR

1 white cabbage
1 tablespoon sea salt
½ teaspoon caraway seeds (optional)
½ teaspoon mustard seeds (optional)

GOES WITH
Cheese Toastie with Tomato Chutney (page 34), Cannellini Bean and Parsley Dip (page 156), Leek, Cavolo Nero and White Bean Soup (page 61), My Mum's Braised Lentils with Salsa Rossa (page 106), Hugo's Röstis with Green Sauce and Poached Eggs (page 112)

Remove the outer leaves of the cabbage and discard them. Slice the cabbage thinly, using a mandoline if you have one, but being careful with your fingers. Put the shredded cabbge into a large bowl with the salt and spices, if using. Massage the cabbage with your hands for about 3 minutes – this is how the fermentation process will begin. As you massage, the cabbage should start producing liquid and start to break down. Tightly pack the cabbage into a sterilised 500ml (17oz) jar (see intro), using the back of a spoon to push it down. You want the cabbage to be fully submerged under the liquid.

Put the lid on the jar and leave it in a cool, dry spot in your kitchen, out of direct sunlight, for at least 5 days. Check the sauerkraut every few days, tasting it and maybe pushing the cabbage back down under the liquid if needed. You'll know it's ready when the salty flavour has been replaced with a tangy, fermented one. You can leave it for a longer or shorter time depending on what flavour profile you'd like it to have. Once opened, store in the refrigerator for as long as you like.

Rosemary and Garlic Chips

These are the perfect side for almost any meal. I started making these during lockdown for my family, and still love making them for me and Hugo. Adding the rosemary and garlic later on in the cooking process is key to making sure they don't burn but still add lots of flavour to the chips (French fries). Fluffing the potatoes up before they go into the oven helps the chips get nice and crispy. I use rapeseed (canola) oil because it has a higher smoke point than olive oil, which means it can be heated to a higher temperature without losing its nutrients and flavour.

SERVES 4

1kg (2lb 4oz) Maris Piper potatoes (or another floury variety), peeled and cut into chips (French fries)
6 tablespoons rapeseed (canola) oil
1 tablespoon plain (all-purpose) flour
5 garlic cloves, finely chopped
5–6 sprigs of rosemary, leaves finely chopped
sea salt

GOES WITH
Slow-cooked Ratatouille (page 136), Hugo's Gem Lettuce Caesar Salad (page 126), Tomato Chutney (page 154), Poached Pears with Cream (page 174)

Preheat the oven to 220°C fan (425°F).

Put the chips into a large saucepan of very generously salted cold water. Place the pan over a high heat and bring the water to the boil. You are only parboiling the potatoes, so as soon as the water comes to the boil, take the pan off the heat and drain the potatoes. If you cook the potatoes for too long, they will lose their shape and become one big hot mess. I've learnt that the hard way before!

Drain the potatoes thoroughly and leave them to cool in the colander for a couple of minutes. Then, shake the colander a couple of times to fluff the potatoes: this will help them crisp up in the oven, but don't shake the colander too vigorously or you might break them. Tip the potatoes into a bowl and toss through the oil, flour and a generous pinch of sea salt. Mix everything well.

Tip the chips onto a baking tray (pan) lined with baking parchment. Make sure that they are evenly distributed because the more space they have, the more evenly they will colour. Use two baking trays if you need to.

Cook the chips in the oven for 50–60 minutes until they are deliciously crispy and golden, moving them around the tray halfway through. About 10 minutes before the chips are ready, take the tray out and add the garlic and rosemary, then give everything a good mix and return the chips to the oven to finish cooking.

Once they are ready, tip the chips into a bowl, add a good pinch of salt, mix and serve piping hot.

Tomato Chutney

When I was living in Wales and growing my own vegetables, I used to make a big batch of this at the end of the summer when I still had a huge amount of tomatoes ripening in the greenhouse but I didn't know what to do with them. The process of making chutney is slow, so it's good for a Sunday or a quiet evening in. It's always a good thing to have in the refrigerator to elevate a snack plate or sandwich, or just to have with cheese and crackers. A jar of chutney also makes a lovely gift for a friend. When making jams, pickles or chutneys, it's really important to make sure your jar is sterilised. Wash the jar with warm soapy water, then pour the contents of a kettle full of boiling water over the inside, outside and tops of the jar. Dry it with a clean dish towel and set aside.

SERVES 4 PEOPLE

5 red onions, sliced
4 tablespoons extra virgin
   olive oil
6 star anise
12 cloves
4 cardamom pods
3kg (6lb 10oz) tomatoes,
   roughly diced (any variety
   will do)
200g (7oz/scant 1 cup) caster
   (superfine) sugar
8 tablespoons red wine
   vinegar
sea salt and freshly ground
   black pepper

GOES WITH
*Warm Lentil Salad with
Smoked Almonds and Feta
(page 131), Baked Eggs
(page 31), Caramelised Leeks,
Toasted Walnuts and Fried
Eggs on Toast (page 42)*

Put the onions into a large heavy-based saucepan with the olive oil, star anise, cloves and cardamom pods. Season with sea salt and then cook over a low heat for about 10 minutes.

Add the diced tomatoes, sugar, vinegar and salt and pepper and increase the heat to medium.

Leave the chutney to cook for 2–3 hours over a low-medium heat, stirring regularly. It will initially become watery and will then begin to thicken and reduce. Take it off the heat once it has reduced by about three-quarters and the texture is jammy.

Store in a sterilised jar in the refrigerator and it'll keep for a few weeks.

Crispy Breadcrumbs

I love making these, particularly to sprinkle on top of pasta. I'm definitely driven by texture with food, and the addition of these crispy breadcrumbs adds a crunch to vegetarian dishes that have the tendency to be quite soft. These will last a couple of days in the refrigerator, so make a batch and use them on a few meals. Add to salads in place of croutons or on top of soups or pasta.

SERVES 4 PEOPLE

3 slices of bread
3 tablespoons extra virgin
   olive oil
generous pinch of sea salt

GOES WITH
*Squash, Carrot and Miso Soup
(page 53), Roasted Tomato
Rigatoni with Confit Garlic
and Burrata (page 100),
Roasted Tomato, Thyme and
Butter Bean Soup (page 62)*

Preheat the oven to 210°C (410°F). Drizzle the bread with the oil and place onto a baking tray (pan). Sprinkle generously with salt and then toast in the oven for 10 minutes. Check after 5 minutes and turn over the slices, being careful not to let them burn.

Once toasted, remove from the oven and allow the toast to cool completely. Roughly slice the cooled toast and transfer to a food processor, then pulse until you have coarse breadcrumbs, watching carefully that they don't become too fine. Tip the breadcrumbs into an airtight container and store in the refrigerator. You can add fresh herbs, garlic or whatever you'd desire to the breadcrumbs before you serve them.

Cannellini Bean and Parsley Dip

This is a recipe that I created out of a desire for a dip that felt a little different to the hummus that I was making on repeat. I love adding herbs to dishes as not only do they add flavour, but also freshness and colour. Parsley is a strong herb, so feel free to reduce the quantity if you would like. I often use the addition of cold water in my dips and dressings to create a smoother consistency.

SERVES 6

¼ bunch of fresh flat-leaf parsley, leaves roughly chopped, plus extra to serve
2 × 400g (14oz) tins of cannellini beans, drained and rinsed
2 tablespoons extra virgin olive oil, plus extra to serve
juice of ½ lemon
2 tablespoons cold water
sea salt and freshly ground black pepper
crackers, crisps (chips) or raw vegetables, to serve

GOES WITH
Leeks with Roasted Garlic And Walnut Sauce (page 140), Crispy Kale (page 144), Pickled Summer Vegetables (page 146), Confit Garlic (page 149), Crispy Breadcrumbs (page 155)

Put everything into a food processor and blend until smooth. Check the seasoning, then serve the dip piled onto a plate with crackers, crisps (chips) or raw vegetables. Finish with a drizzle of olive oil and a sprinkling of parsley.

Puddings

158–183

During the pandemic, I took an online pastry course taught by two extraordinary bakers, Ravneet Gill and Nicola Lamb. My fascination with pastry developed off the back of my interest in baking bread, and – surprisingly, as someone who had not grasped science at all at school – the science of it all gripped me. A few years later, I spent a month working in the kitchen at The Pig hotel in Kent, south-eastern England, with a week spent in the pastry section. Safe to say I was hooked. I thrived on the order and structure of it all; by nature, I am quite a rushed person and I love that pastry forces me to slow down and really focus on every step I am taking. There is not much room for error in this kind of cooking.

When it comes to creating puddings (desserts) for my supper clubs, I enjoy using them as a way to express myself as a cook and baker. I like to finish with a not-so-serious pudding that can be enjoyed on big sharing plates like the rest of the menu. I relish in creating something that's playful and possibly a bit over the top, such as the Meringue Tower (page 166), inspired by Jeremy Lee, the chef proprietor of Quo Vadis in London. This chimes with the type of energy that I'm trying to create for the evening. When hosting, it's critical to make the pudding in advance and leave only the very finishing touches or the plating to the last minute. When you've served your main and probably been on your feet preparing everything for at least a few hours, all you really want to do is put the pudding in a bowl and serve it. Have fun with how you present these puddings, play around, and my general rule is that whipped cream makes almost any pudding better.

No-churn Raspberry Ice Cream

A few years ago, I invested in an ice cream machine and have used it hundreds of times since. I normally always have a tub of homemade ice cream in the freezer for either myself or friends when they come round, and I make it a lot when I host supper clubs too. I felt that I couldn't not have an ice cream recipe in this book because I talk endlessly about how much I love making it, so I've created one that you don't need an ice cream maker for.

SERVES 6 PEOPLE

250g (9oz) raspberries
95g (3¼oz/generous ⅓ cup) caster (superfine) sugar
1 tablespoon water
500ml (17 fl oz/generous 2 cups) double (heavy) cream
250ml (8 fl oz/1 cup) whole (full-fat) milk
½ teaspoon vanilla extract

GOES WITH
Tomatoes on Toast (page 28), White Miso Butter Beans (page 65), Tomato, Aubergine and Mozzarella Lasagne (page 85), Slow-cooked Ratatouille (page 136)

First, make the raspberry sauce, which you will mix through the ice cream later. Put the raspberries, 15g (½oz) of the sugar and the water into a saucepan over a low heat. Cover and cook the berries for 5–10 minutes until soft and broken down, stirring occasionally.

Remove the pan from the heat and use a hand-held blender to blend the raspberries to a smooth sauce, then set aside to cool. Once cool, pass the sauce through a sieve into a bowl, discarding the seeds.

In a separate bowl, combine the cream, milk, the remaining sugar and the vanilla extract. Whisk together until the sugar has fully dissolved. You could do this step in a stand mixer using the whisk attachment if you prefer. Pour the mixture into an airtight container and freeze for 45 minutes.

After 45 minutes, stir the mixture gently for a couple of minutes before putting it back in the freezer. Repeat this process at least twice more, preferably three times. The last time you take it out of the freezer to mix, evenly dot 6 teaspoons of the raspberry sauce on top of the ice cream, then push the handle of the teaspoon to the bottom of the tub and join up each blob of raspberry sauce until you have created a swirl pattern in the ice cream. Repeat this swirling process once more with 6 more dots of raspberry sauce in roughly the same places as the first round. Refrigerate overnight, if possible, or for a few hours. If you have any sauce left, keep it covered in the refrigerator to serve later with the ice cream.

I'd recommend taking the ice cream out of the freezer about 10 minutes before you want to serve it. Scoop it into bowls and serve it with any leftover raspberry sauce.

Chocolate Chip and Almond Butter Cookies

I'm such a sucker for almond butter and wanted to incorporate that nutty flavour into my cookie recipe. These are so quick to make, which makes them ideal if you want an easy afternoon pick-me-up or to surprise a friend. I love making the cookies for pudding (dessert) when I'm hosting, served with a scoop of vanilla ice cream. If you want to do this, you can make the cookie dough in advance and bake them to serve. You could also use the No-churn Raspberry Ice Cream recipe on page 162 and just leave out the berries.

MAKES 10–12 COOKIES

100g (3½oz) unsalted butter, at room temperature
150g (5½oz/scant 1¼ cups) plain (all-purpose) flour
50g (1¾oz/scant ¼ cup) caster (superfine) sugar
50g (1¾oz/generous ¼ cup) light brown soft sugar
1 teaspoon sea salt, plus extra for sprinking
2 tablespoons smooth almond butter
¼ teaspoon baking powder
1 medium egg
100g (3½oz) dark (bittersweet) chocolate with at least 70% cocoa solids, roughly chopped (you want some bigger and some smaller pieces)

GOES WITH
Baked Beans on Toast (page 41), Coconut and Mushroom Broth with Soba Noodles (page 57), Courgette and Red Pepper Stew with Buffalo Mozzarella and Almonds (page 71), Roasted Tomato Rigatoni with Confit Garlic and Burrata (page 100)

Combine all the ingredients except for the chocolate in a bowl and mix until smooth. Using either a food processor or a hand-held electric mixer will speed up this process, so I'd recommend using one. Mix through the chocolate, then tip out the dough onto a large sheet of baking parchment and roll it into a thick sausage shape, roughly 5cm (2 inches) in diameter, twisting the baking paper at the ends to secure the dough. Refrigerate the cookie dough for about 2 hours.

Preheat the oven to 175°C (350°F) and line two baking sheets with baking parchment.

Roll the cookie dough into 10–12 balls and lay them out on the prepared baking sheets, spreading them well apart. Chill in the refrigerator for at least an hour. Bake in the oven for 10–15 minutes until golden brown. Sprinkle the cookies with sea salt as soon as you remove them from the oven. Leave them to cool on the baking sheets for 5 minutes, then transfer them to a wire rack to cool completely – but if you can't resist, feel free to eat them while they are still warm!

Meringue Tower

Meringues are generally tricky to get right. I have had many failures for many different reasons when I've attempted to make them, but it's never been enough to put me off. In fact, the reason why I love making meringue towers so much is precisely because they can be imperfect. If your meringues are in any way 'imperfect' when you remove them from the oven, just use the cream and fruit to cover up the imperfections. I highly recommend using a stand mixer for this recipe, as I don't think you'll ever get the right consistency by hand. You can make the meringues in advance, but I wouldn't assemble the meringue tower until you're ready to serve.

SERVES 6 PEOPLE

6 medium egg whites
380g (13½oz/1⅔ cups) caster (superfine) sugar
60g (2oz/¼ cup) crème fraîche
220ml (7½ fl oz/scant 1 cup) double (heavy) cream
300g (10½oz) mixed berries of your choice

FOR THE BERRY SAUCE
250g (9oz) raspberries or strawberries, hulled
1 tablespoon caster (superfine) sugar
50ml (1¾ fl oz/3½ tablespoons) water

GOES WITH
Burnt Courgette, Basil and Cannellini Bean Stew (page 54), Hugo's Gem Lettuce Caesar Salad (page 126), Labneh with Roasted Tomatoes, Thyme and Confit Garlic (page 139), Leeks with Roasted Garlic and Walnut Sauce (page 140)

Preheat the oven to 100°C (215°F) and line two baking sheets with baking parchment.

Put the egg whites into the bowl of a stand mixer and, using the balloon whisk attachment, whisk the eggs on a low setting for 4 minutes. Next, increase the speed to medium and start to add the sugar, 1 tablespoon at a time. Keep whisking on a medium speed for 15–20 minutes until the meringue is silky and firm and when you hold the bowl upside down you are completely confident that it'll stay in place. It's really important that you've whisked the whites for long enough.

Spread the mixture out into 5–6 circles on the prepared baking sheets. Make sure there are a couple that are slightly bigger, as they will act as the foundations of the tower. A variety of sizes will be good for the final look. Put the meringues into the oven and immediately turn down the heat to 80°C (175°F). Bake the meringues for 1½ hours, then turn off the oven and leave them in there for at least 2 hours, or overnight if possible. This helps them set.

While the meringues are cooking, make the berry sauce. Combine all the ingredients in a saucepan over a medium heat and cook for about 10 minutes, stirring occasionally, until the berries have softened and broken down. Remove the pan from the heat and set aside to cool. Once cooled, feel free to pass through a sieve and muslin cloth if you want a smoother texture without the seeds. When you're ready to assemble the meringue towers, combine the crème fraîche and cream in the clean bowl of the stand mixer and use the balloon whisk attachment to whisk until lightly whipped. Place the larger meringues on a serving plate, then, using the cream as glue, pile the meringues up with cream, with the raspberry sauce in between.

Top the tower with a smaller meringue, followed by a last dollop of cream and berry sauce, then stick the berries of your choice to the cream wherever you'd like on the tower. Don't worry if the tower feels a bit messy, that's the point! Serve immediately.

Apple and Blackberry Pie

There's something about making a pie that will always feel nostalgic and comforting. It's definitely the pudding (dessert) that I enjoy making the most, because I love how the process forces me to be patient and the outcome is just so rewarding. I have provided a recipe for homemade pastry below – you could buy the pastry, but I recommend trying to make it yourself as it really is so simple and such a rewarding process. I like using Royal Gala apples in pies because they are not overly sweet, but use what you prefer or whatever is available in the shops.

SERVES 6–8 PEOPLE

FOR THE PASTRY
250g (9oz) very cold unsalted
   butter, plus extra for
   greasing
300g (10½oz/scant 1½ cups)
   plain (all-purpose) flour,
   plus extra for dusting
30g (1oz/2 heaped
   tablespoons) caster
   (superfine) sugar
6–7 tablespoons ice-cold
   water

FOR THE FILLING
juice of 1 lemon
12 crisp eating (dessert)
   apples, such as Royal Gala
1 tablespoon cornflour
   (cornstarch)
60g (2oz/generous ¼ cup)
   caster (superfine) sugar
350g (12oz) blackberries
50ml (1¾ fl oz/3½
   tablespoons) water
1 cinnamon stick
1 medium egg, beaten
demerara sugar, for
   sprinkling
custard, to serve

An hour before you want to make the pastry, cut the cold butter into roughly 1.5cm (½ inch) cubes and then refrigerate it until you are ready.

To make the pastry, put the flour and sugar into a food processor, add the butter and then pulse until the mixture resembles breadcrumbs – be careful not to overwork it. Add the water 1 tablespoon at a time, pulsing to combine between each addition, until the dough comes together. Turn it out onto a lightly floured surface and shape it into a ball. Flatten the ball into a 3cm (1¼ inch) thick circle and wrap it in cling film (plastic wrap), then chill in the refrigerator for 1 hour.

Meanwhile, make the filling. Fill a bowl with water and add half the lemon juice. Peel, core and quarter the apples, putting them into the bowl of water as you go. This will stop the apples from discolouring. When all the apples are done, drain them, pat them dry and thinly slice them into a bowl. Add the cornflour and 2 teaspoons of the caster sugar and mix everything gently to combine. It's best to do this with your hands, even if it is a little messy. Once the apples are coated in the cornflour and sugar, cook them in a deep saucepan with a lid over a low heat for about ten minutes, stirring regularly.

Separately, put the blackberries into a saucepan with the water, cinnamon stick, the rest of the lemon juice and the remaining sugar. Cook over a low-medium heat for about 15 minutes until the berries have started to break down and you're left with a lovely berry sauce. Remove from the heat and allow to cool slightly, you can sift the blackberry sauce to remove the seeds but if the seeds don't bother you then leave them in. Remove the cinnamon stick and then pour the sauce over the apples and mix so that the apples are coated.

CONTINUED OVERLEAF

GOES WITH
Tofu 'Meatballs' with a Simple Tomato Sauce (page 104), My Mum's Braised Lentils with Salsa Rossa (page 106), Warm Lentil Salad with Smoked Almonds and Feta (page 131), Smoky Squash Stew with Spinach (page 76)

Grease a 26cm (10 inch), deep pie dish with butter, then remove the chilled pastry from the refrigerator. Cut off one-third of the pastry, then wrap it up again and return it to the refrigerator.

Shape the rest of the dough back into a ball, then, on a lightly floured surface, flatten the ball of dough into a disc with the heel of your hand. Flour the top and roll it out into a circle big enough to fit the pie dish with some overhang. Roll the pastry gently over the rolling pin and lift it over the dish. Carefully drop it in place by rolling it off the rolling pin, making sure that you centralise it. Use your fingertips to gently push the pastry into the edges of the pie dish. Leave the overhang as you will use it to fold over the ends of the lattice. Put the pie dish into the refrigerator to chill for 1 hour.

Now make the strips for your lattice, which will go on the top of the pie. Remove the remaining pastry from the refrigerator and shape it into a ball. Roll it out on a lightly floured surface into a circle a bit smaller than the pie dish. Cut the pastry into 10 strips about 2cm (¾ inch) wide. Remember that the strips can be slightly different sizes depending on the part of the pie they'll be covering. Lay the strips on a baking sheet lined with baking parchment and refrigerate them until the pie is filled.

Spoon the filling into the chilled pastry case. To create the lattice, place five strips of pastry vertically across the pie, leaving a space of about 2cm (¾ inch) between each strip. Then weave the other five strips horizontally across the first ones, until most of the filling is covered and you have a lovely criss-cross pattern on the top of the pie. To secure the lattice, fold the overhanging pastry in on itself so that the strips are secured underneath. You can create a nice pattern around the edge of the pie using your fingers to do this, so that the pie will end up having a crinkled crust. Refrigerate the pie for a final 30 minutes.

Preheat the oven to 180°C (350°F). Remove the pie from the refrigerator and brush the top with the beaten egg, then sprinkle with the demerara sugar. Bake the pie in the oven for 30–40 minutes until the pastry is golden. Remove from the oven and allow to cool slightly, then enjoy with custard.

Chocolate Mousse and Whipped Cream

Chocolate mousse is an iconic pudding for a reason. It is ideal for hosting because you can make it in advance and then just serve it straight from the refrigerator when you're ready to go. It's fun to serve it in a big bowl and let everyone help themselves. Chocolate goes so beautifully with extra virgin olive oil and sea salt, so if you are feeling fancy, add them at the end too.

SERVES 4 PEOPLE

90g (3¼oz) dark (bittersweet) chocolate with at least 70% cocoa solids, roughly chopped
60g (2oz) unsalted butter
a pinch of sea salt, plus extra to serve
3 medium egg whites
60g (2oz/generous ¼ cup) caster (superfine) sugar
200ml (7 fl oz/scant 1 cup) double (heavy) cream
4 tablespoons extra virgin olive oil (optional)

GOES WITH
Ribollita (page 72), Squash and Mascarpone Fusilli (page 109)

Put the chocolate, butter and salt into a heatproof bowl and set it over a saucepan of simmering water, ensuring the bottom of the bowl doesn't touch the water. Stir occasionally until the chocolate and butter have both melted, then remove from the heat and set aside to cool.

Put the egg whites and sugar into the bowl of a stand mixer and, using the balloon whisk attachment, whisk them slowly before increasing the speed for a couple of minutes until the whites form stiff peaks. Gently scrape the mixture into a bowl.

Clean the bowl of the stand mixer and, using the balloon whisk attachment again, whip the cream very gently on a low speed, just so that it thickens slightly. This should take no more than 30–60 seconds – watch it carefully. However, if you are making the mousse to chill overnight and serve the following day, only use half of the cream for the mousse, using the other half fresh the next day to serve with the mousse, as whipped cream is generally better made fresh.

Next, very gently fold the egg whites into the chocolate, one spoonful at a time. Your main aim is to keep the air in the egg whites, as this is what will make the mousse light and fluffy, so work delicately. Once all the egg whites are incorporated, gently fold in half the whipped cream, making sure not to overwork the mixture. Set the rest of the whipped cream aside for when you are ready to serve the mousse.

Refrigerate the mousse for at least 1 hour, or longer if possible. You could make this the night before you serve it, so that it's completely ready to go if you're hosting and want to get ahead.

Once set, serve in bowls with a spoonful of whipped cream, a sprinkle of sea salt and a drizzle of extra virgin olive oil, if using.

Poached Pears with Cream

I first served this at a supper club, when I was cooking with my friend Tom, and I've made it many times at home since. The poached pears are a good staple to get to know as they can be used in so many ways across different dishes. For example, they'd be great with yoghurt and granola for breakfast or with the chocolate mousse on page 172. If you're not making them to host people, you can store them in an airtight container in the refrigerator with their poaching liquid for a few days.

SERVES 4 PEOPLE

1.5 litres (50¾ fl oz/6⅓ cups)
    water
350g (12oz/1½ cups) caster
    (superfine) sugar
12 cloves
6 star anise
1 teaspoon ground cinnamon
    or 1 cinnamon stick
6 Conference (or Bosc) pears
60ml (2 fl oz / ¼ cup) double
    (heavy) cream

GOES WITH
*Burnt Courgette, Basil and
Cannellini Bean Stew (page
54), Chicory, Apple, Celery
and Blue Cheese Salad (page
122), Leeks with Roasted
Garlic and Walnut Sauce
(page 140)*

Pour the water into a large saucepan, then whisk in the sugar, cloves, star anise and cinnamon. The ground cinnamon can be a bit messy, but it adds a really lovely colour to the pears. If you don't want a mess, just add a stick instead. Heat gently and stir until all the sugar has dissolved, then remove the pan from the heat.

Peel the pears, leaving the stalks on, and put them straight into the pan with the poaching liquid. If you leave them out for too long, they will go brown, so get them straight into the liquid once you've peeled each one. I would recommend cutting a piece of baking paper the same size as the pan, covering the pears with it. If the pears aren't covered in this way they may start to brown on the edges that aren't fully submerged.

Once all the pears are in the pan, bring it to a simmer over a medium heat, then reduce the heat to low. Simmer for 15–20 minutes until the pears are soft and the flesh has started to look slightly translucent.

If you're not serving the pears straightaway, leave them to cool in the poaching liquid and then transfer everything to an airtight container and store in the refrigerator. Otherwise, take the pears out of the liquid, lay them on their side and cut off about 1cm (½ inch) from the bottom, so that the bottom is flat. This is so that the pears will stand up on the plates – I think this is a really fun way to serve them.

When you are ready to serve, spoon just enough cream onto each plate to cover the surface, then stand a pear up in the centre of each plate.

Brown Butter Apple Tarte Tatin

There's nothing quite like an apple tarte tatin, and I love making it with brown butter as it just elevates it that bit further. This is one of the few pudding recipes in this book that I'd suggest not making in advance, as the fresher it is the better, but using pre-made puff pastry means it's very quick to put together.

SERVES 8 PEOPLE

plain (all-purpose) flour,
  for dusting
320g (11¼oz) shop-bought
  puff pastry
45g (1½oz) unsalted butter
65g (2¼oz/generous ¼ cup)
  golden caster (superfine)
  sugar
4 crisp eating apples, peeled,
  quartered, cored and thinly
  sliced
pinch of sea salt
1 medium egg, beaten
whipped cream, to serve

GOES WITH
*Wild Mushrooms, Butter Beans
and Parsley Salsa on Toast
(page 32), Tomato, Aubergine
and Mozzarella Lasagne
(page 85), Warm Lentil Salad
with Smoked Almonds and
Feta (page 131)*

Preheat the oven to 200°C (400°F).

Roll out the pastry on a lightly floured surface to about 3mm (⅛ inch) thick. Using a plate as a guide, cut out a 20cm (8 inch) circle and lay it on a sheet of baking parchment, then put it in the refrigerator to chill while you prepare everything else.

Place a 20cm (8 inch) ovenproof frying pan over a medium heat and add the butter. Stir it occasionally for about 5 minutes until it is frothing, brown specks have started to appear on the bottom and it smells slightly caramelised. Watch it carefully and as soon as it has browned, remove it from the heat. Stir in 50g (1¾oz/scant ¼ cup) of the sugar and keep simmering until it has turned to caramel, which should take about 2 minutes.

Layer the apple slices onto the caramel, pressing them down gently and making a neat pattern with all the slices facing the same way. You should get about three layers of apples. Once all the apple slices are in place, sprinkle with the remaining sugar. Place the pan back over a low-medium heat and let the apples cook gently in the caramel butter for 10–15 minutes until they have started to soften. Remove the pan from the heat and leave to stand for 5 minutes.

Take the pastry circle out of the refrigerator and place it on top of the apples, tucking the edges in and pressing the pastry gently onto the apples.

Brush the top with the beaten egg. You will be flipping the tart to serve it, so you won't see the top, but I like the texture that the egg wash gives the pastry.

Cook the tart in the oven for 15–20 minutes, or until the pastry is golden and puffed up. Once cooked, remove it from the oven and gently run a palette knife around the edge of the pan to unstick any bits that might have stuck. Leave it to stand for 5 minutes, then cover the pan with a serving plate and confidently flip the pan and plate over. Slice and serve immediately with whipped cream.

Flourless Chocolate Cake

This is a really dense, rich cake that goes perfectly with a dollop of crème fraîche. It's normal for the cake to collapse a little bit as it cools down, since it doesn't have the flour in it to produce a springy centre, so don't worry when that happens. I love this in the winter when there's a shortage of fruit in season. As with the chocolate mousse recipe on page 172, it's important to keep as much air in the eggs as possible.

SERVES 8 PEOPLE

120g (4¼oz) dark
  (bittersweet) chocolate with
  at least 70% cocoa solids,
  chopped
120g (4¼oz) unsalted butter,
  cubed, plus extra for
  greasing
pinch of sea salt
3 tablespoons cocoa
  (unsweetened chocolate)
  powder
1 teaspoon vanilla extract
1 teaspoon baking powder
4 medium eggs
120g (4¼oz/generous ½ cup)
  caster (superfine) sugar
crème fraîche, to serve

GOES WITH

*Miso Aubergines, Sushi Rice
and Smashed Cucumber Salad
(page 110), Tomato, Aubergine
and Mozzarella Lasagne (page
85), Wild Mushrooms, Butter
Beans and Parsley Salsa on
Toast (page 32)*

Preheat the oven to 150°C (300°F) and grease a 20cm (8 inch) cake tin (pan).

Put the chocolate, butter and salt into a heatproof bowl and set it over a saucepan of simmering water, ensuring the bottom of the bowl doesn't touch the water. Stir occasionally until the chocolate and butter have both melted, then remove from the heat. Sift in 2 tablespoons of the cocoa powder, then add the vanilla extract and baking powder and stir until combined.

Put the eggs and sugar into the bowl of a stand mixer and beat them until they are pale yellow, thickened and bubbly, about 5 minutes.

Fold the eggs and sugar into the chocolate mixture a spoonful at a time using a spatula, being careful to keep as much air in the eggs as possible.

Pour the cake batter into the prepared tin, then bake in the oven for about 45 minutes–1 hour.

Remove from the oven and allow to cool completely in the tin, then remove the cake from the tin and sift the remaining tablespoon of cocoa powder evenly over the top. Slice and serve with a dollop of crème fraîche.

Store, covered, in the refrigerator. This cake is still lovely (maybe even better) the next day served cold.

Blood Orange and Thyme Cake

Blood oranges are such a delightful fruit. They signify a glimmer of hope in the middle of what is usually a long and miserable winter, and are also unbelievably beautiful – I love how strong they look in any dish, sweet or savoury. You can make this cake with ordinary oranges (like in this picture) if you want to make it out of blood orange season, of course. I think it works particularly well if you're hosting for lunch, as for some reason it feels more like a day cake than evening.

SERVES 8 PEOPLE

200g (7oz) unsalted butter,
    at room temperature
200g (7oz/1 cup minus
    2 tablespoons) caster
    (superfine) sugar
2 medium eggs
200g (7oz/1 ⅔ cups) plain
    (all-purpose) flour
1 teaspoon baking powder
zest and juice of 2 blood
    oranges
1 teaspoon vanilla extract

FOR THE ICING
250g (9oz) cream cheese
60ml (2 fl oz/¼ cup) double
    (heavy) cream
40g (1½oz/⅓ cup) icing
    (powdered) sugar, sifted
1 teaspoon vanilla extract
zest of 2 blood oranges plus
    juice of 1
3 sprigs of fresh thyme,
    leaves picked

TO DECORATE
½ blood orange, sliced

GOES WITH
*Whipped Ricotta and
Asparagus Bruschetta (page
37), Roasted Tomato, Thyme
and Butter Bean Soup (page 62)*

Preheat the oven to 160°C (325°F). Grease a 20cm (8 inch) round tin and line with baking parchment.

Cream the butter and sugar together in a stand mixer fitted with the paddle attachment until they are light and pale. Scrape down the sides of the bowl, then add the eggs one at a time along with a tablespoon of flour with each egg. This will stop the mixture curdling. Continue mixing until all the eggs are thoroughly incorporated, scraping down the sides of the bowl again if necessary.

Add the baking powder to the remaining flour and mix it through. Remove the bowl from the stand mixer and scrape any batter off the paddle. Fold the flour and baking powder gently into the batter, a tablespoon at a time. Once all the flour is incorporated, stir in the orange zest and juice, along with the vanilla extract.

Pour the batter into the prepared tin, smoothing the top of the cake with your spatula, then bake in the oven for 45–50 minutes until a skewer inserted into the centre comes out clean. Remove from the oven and leave to cool completely on a wire rack.

While the cake is baking, make the icing. Combine all the ingredients except the thyme in the bowl of a stand mixer and beat until the icing is a spreadable consistency. Don't be tempted to over-beat it, as this will make your icing stodgy and hard to spread nicely. Add half the thyme leaves to the icing and mix them in gently, reserving the other half to decorate the cake with. Cover the bowl and refrigerate until you are ready to ice the cake.

Once the cake has cooled, remove it from the tin and transfer it to a plate. Spread the icing evenly over the top of the cake, then decorate it with slices of blood orange and the reserved thyme leaves. Any leftovers can be stored in an airtight container in the refrigerator for 2–3 days.

Peach, Hazelnut and Basil Galette

A galette is basically a simpler version of a tart, and I love it for that reason. You may have realised by now that I love pastry, and this is a great way to experiment with it if you're not that confident yet. This recipe combines a few of my favourite things, with nuts and fruit and then basil bringing a bit of savoury to what would otherwise be a very sweet pudding. I macerate the fruit in the basil and sugar syrup overnight, but you could also do this just for an hour or so to get a similar effect. As with most puddings (desserts), this is perfect with a spoonful of lightly whipped cream.

SERVES 6 PEOPLE

4 peaches, halved, stoned and thickly sliced
½ bunch of fresh basil, leaves picked, plus extra to serve
100g (3½oz/scant ½ cup) caster (superfine) sugar
juice of ½ lemon
60g (2oz/scant ½ cup) blanched hazelnuts
1 × quantity shortcrust pastry (page 169), made with 40g (1½oz) caster (superfine) sugar (or use shop-bought)
1 medium egg, beaten
3 tablespoons demerara sugar
whipped cream, to serve

GOES WITH
Miso Aubergines, Sushi Rice and Smashed Cucumber Salad (page 110), Slow-cooked Ratatouille (page 136), Simple Slaw (page 143)

Put the peach slices and basil leaves into a bowl.

Sprinkle the sugar and squeeze the lemon the over the peaches and basil, then cover the bowl and set aside to macerate for a few hours, or preferably overnight.

When you're ready to cook, preheat the oven to 160°C fan (325°F) and line a baking tray (pan) with baking parchment. Place the baking tray that you're going to cook the galette on in the oven while it heats up, which will help you get a lovely crispy base on the galette.

Put the hazelnuts onto another baking tray and toast them in the oven for 5 minutes, keeping a close eye on them. Take them out and set aside to cool.

To assemble the galette, place the pastry on a lightly floured surface and flatten it into a disc with the heel of your hand. Flour the top, then roll it out into a circle roughly 30cm (12 inches) wide. Take the hot baking tray out of the oven and carefully transfer the pastry to the baking tray.

Drain the peaches and basil in a colander, then place them neatly in the centre of the pastry, leaving about 5cm (2 inches) around the edge. Fold the sides of the pastry over the peaches. Brush the pastry with the beaten egg, then sprinkle it with the demarara sugar.

Bake the galette for about 45 minutes until golden and crisp, checking it after 30 minutes. While the galette is baking, roughly chop the hazelnuts.

Remove the galette from the oven and scatter over the hazelnuts while it's warm. Serve with fresh basil leaves and a dollop of whipped cream.

WINTER LUNCH

Wild Mushrooms, Butter Beans
and Parsley Salsa on Toast

Leek and Squash Quiche

Crispy Kale

Brown Butter Apple Tarte Tatin

SPRING SUPPER

Whipped Ricotta and Asparagus Bruschetta

Tofu 'Meatballs' with a Simple Tomato Sauce

Slow-cooked Ratatouille

Hugo's Caesar Gem Lettuce Salad

No-churn Raspberry Ice Cream

SUMMER LUNCH

Gazpacho

Roasted Aubergine, Tahini Sauce and
Cucumber Salsa on Toast

Cold Noodle Salad with Tahini and Miso Dressing

Chocolate Chip and Almond Butter Cookies

AUTUMN SUPPER

Caramelised Leeks, Toasted
Walnuts and Fried Eggs on Toast

Lentil and Mushroom Bolognese

Poached Pears with Cream

STAY FOR SUPPER

XANTHE is a cook and supper club host based in London. Her passion is to show people that food should fundamentally be enjoyed, through every step of the cooking, plating and eating process. She spent six years living in Wales and growing her own food, which has spurred her to continue to highlight the abundance of beautiful produce available to cook with, where vegetables can be the main part of the plate.

ACKNOWLEDGEMENTS

Thank you to each person who has attended my supper clubs from the very early days until now. You have encouraged me to continue and to keep pushing with them even when I was feeling like I didn't have the capacity to continue. To everyone who has followed me on social media and sent words, messages and comments of support in moments of highs and lows, you are also why I am here today writing these words and I couldn't be more grateful for you sticking with me through the years.

I want to thank my parents, Charlie and Caroline. You have nurtured me my whole life and allowed me to be exactly who I wanted to be. Everything I've expressed an interest in doing you have encouraged me to pursue and in moments where I was clearly so lost and struggling, you've always noticed even when I didn't think it was obvious and empathetically suggested a change in direction. There's absolutely no way this book would exist without the support of you two. Mumma, an even more special thank you to you for testing the recipes in this book. I will never be able to express my gratitude but I am so grateful that you not only spent days on days testing, but on top of that your cooking throughout my life has shaped the way I cook too. So, I hope you can see yourself and your impact on me through everything I cook.

To Damian, my friend and mentor who from the beginning has taught me so much about food and cooking, how to respect ingredients and care for them so that they taste incredible on the plate, but most importantly for always nurturing my confidence. Confidence in the kitchen is something I have always struggled with, knowing my place and that I belong, and Damian has always shown me that I did deserve to be there. A constant source of inspiration both from restaurant kitchens in London and cooking on fire pits together in Scotland and Wales, I will forever be indebted to your support.

To Hugo, thank you for your love, guidance and patience in designing this book and for almost ten years of fun and inspiration before. You are the one who really showed me into the world of food nine years ago and there's no way I would be here without you, I love you!

To my siblings Jack, India, Tara, Kinvara and Felix, you guys are my rock and you make me who I am.

Thank you to Emily, my wonderful agent who has given me so much encouragement from before this book existed and to Issy, my editor. Issy, it has been such a pleasure to work with you and I count myself lucky every day. Thank you for believing in me from the beginning. Alannah, thank you for being such a great friend and support through the time of writing this book and before and after.

Thank you to all of my friends who have been there for me throughout moments when I felt quite far away living in Wales, coming to my supper clubs, many words of encouragement, and some of my happiest memories are surrounded by you guys. But especially to Jimmy and Tily, my sisters, I would genuinely be lost without you two.

To A.I PR, DH–PR, Re Agency, Margaret Howell, Ganni, Toast, Story MFG, and Joanna Ling Ceramics, thank you for your contributions to the shoot. Working with brands that I've admired for such a long time on this project has truly been a dream come true.

Lastly but certainly not least, to Ola, working with you on this book has been the greatest joy and our week in France is a time I'll never forget. Thank you for portraying my recipes so beautifully and for your kind and generous spirit. Clare, you know how much I love you and how happy I am to have had you styling this book. You get me and you get my food, and you've made it all look so beautiful as you do with everything. To Poppy, for your work on this book but also for your support cooking on so many of my events and supper clubs, and for our friendship. Laura, our shoot week in France would not have been so seamless without you, and neither would any of the events I've cooked at with you. Working with you is the greatest joy and I hope you know how good you are. Thank you to Martha for your support in France, it was such a dream to spend that time with you and you are so incredible in the kitchen. Jenny and Christophe, you came to the rescue in France with your beautiful produce and pie dishes. Thank you! I am so happy your beautiful radishes and sage are on the cover, from your garden that has inspired me so much.

Thank you again to everyone who has been a part of this journey with me, it truly takes a village!